ERROL, OLIVIA & THE MERRY MEN OF SHERWOOD:
THE MAKING OF THE ADVENTURES OF ROBIN HOOD

RUPERT ALISTAIR

Copyright © 2020
Rupert Alistair
All rights reserved. No part of this publication may be reproduced, distributed, or transmitted in any form or by any means, including photocopying, recording, or other electronic or mechanical methods, without the prior written permission of the publisher, except in the case of brief quotations embodied in critical reviews and certain other noncommercial uses permitted by copyright law.

CONTENTS

LET'S MAKE CAGNEY, ROBIN HOOD! 6

ERROL AND OLIVIA 19

WELCOME TO SHERWOOD! 33

ROBIN AT PLAY 45

TROUBLE AT THE HELM 57

SET IT TO MUSIC AND SEND IT TO THE MASSES 73

LET'S MAKE CAGNEY, ROBIN HOOD!

A full-page ad in an August 1935 issue of *Motion Picture Daily*

In the days when high profile movie stars lunched on a juicy slab of roast beef in their studio's commissary and the guard at the front gate greeted them cordially when they reported for work, the interoffice memo was a powerful and often career-changing slip of paper in Hollywood. The all-mighty moguls of bustling sound stages used memos to rule their domains. In turn, studio bosses received their own share of movie-making correspondence, either as a brief sentence or a lengthy tome, with questions, updates or suggestions from those in their realm. At Warner Brothers, the importance of interoffice memorandum was underscored with a note to all personnel at the bottom of the studio's official printed correspondence sheets: VERBAL MESSAGES CAUSE MISUNDERSTANDING AND DELAYS (PLEASE PUT THEM IN WRITING).

In July 1935, one of these all-important memos was sent by Dwight Franklin, a forty-seven-year-old period costume consultant, working on Warner Brothers' most recent adventure film, *Captain Blood*. The distinguished expert on all things "pirate" sent his memo to the studio's head man, Jack L. Warner, and it would be one of the most significant messages sent in the company's history. It read:

> "Don't you think that Cagney would make a swell Robin Hood? Maybe as a follow up to the [*Midsummer Night's*] *Dream*. With the gang as his Merry Men. [Frank] McHugh, [Allen] Jenkins, [Ross] Alexander, [Hugh] Herbert, etc.
>
> Entirely different from the [1922 Douglas] Fairbanks picture. I have a lot of ideas on this if you are interested."

It was the spark which ignited one of Warners' most elaborate and profitable productions of the decade, although the final product would be worlds apart from Franklin's initial suggestion. The idea of James Cagney as Robin Hood was not as absurd as modern audiences might believe. Franklin's brainstorm was to have a scrappy Robin surrounded by equally world-wise Merry Men, played by his Warner Brothers character actor cronies. The *Dream* referenced by Franklin was Warners' massive effort to bring Shakespeare to the movie screen and prestige to a studio best-known for its fast-paced, gritty gangster pictures.

A Midsummer Night's Dream was the vision of producer Max Reinhardt, whose stage adaption of the Shakespearean classic found great success at the Hollywood Bowl. Warners' film version billed Cagney at the top of a cast featuring many of the studio's most reliable contract players, and gave its star - who was always asking to play a variety of roles - an opportunity to shake off his familiar tough-guy persona. Read in the perspective of the time in which it was sent, Franklin's memo struck Jack Warner as a good idea. As Bottom, the Weaver, in Shakespeare's story, Cagney was required to wear a Robin Hood-style cap, vest and boots, and presented a fairy tale figure alongside his whimsically clad co-stars. Although *A Midsummer Night's Dream* was two months from its release date when the memo was sent, the film was being touted as one of the biggest projects of the decade, and success was expected for it and its star. In addition, the year brought on the actor's debut to the list of Top Ten Moneymakers in Hollywood, boosting the chances of profit for *Dream* and any subsequent Cagney picture.

There were several silent films based on the legendary heroic outlaw, the most recent and famous released in 1922, starring Douglas Fairbanks, Sr. By 1935, Warner Brothers was not the only studio to show interest in producing an updated adaption of the story. In February,

Reliance Pictures - an independent production company who released their films through United Artists - announced their own version of *Robin Hood* to star English actor, Robert Donat. Reliance successfully produced another classic adventure yarn, *The Count of Monte Cristo*, the previous year, launching Donat's leading man career in the United States. The studio wanted to duplicate that success with a similar story featuring the up and coming star. Reliance production chief, Edward Small, disclosed that after completing his current engagement on the London stage, Donat would arrive in Hollywood to begin filming on *Robin Hood*. The project was still in the works as of July but by summer's end Reliance had lost interest, even though much work had been done on research and script drafts.

    Meanwhile, Metro-Goldwin-Mayer, the most prestigious of the big studios in town, had recently scored a hit with *Naughty Marietta*, an operetta that paired singing stars Jeanette MacDonald and Nelson Eddy. Eager for a follow-up film featuring the duo, MGM began developing a musical version of the Robin Hood legend and negotiated a deal with Reliance Pictures for the script treatments, working outline and incomplete draft of its now-abandoned version of the project. Metro also paid $62,500 to the Reginald de Koven estate for the music rights to a late-nineteenth century comic opera based on the legendary bandit. The irony of this transaction was that Jack Warner's company owned the rights to the book and lyric portions of the same opera, which were separate from de Koven's music. Warner purchased the property in the silent era but the idea for a film was shelved after the Douglas Fairbanks picture was successfully made. Now owning the music rights, MGM wanted to obtain Warners' interest in the operetta, and a deal was discussed between the two companies, with a purchase amount of $30,000 being offered.

In August 1935, Warner Brothers began pre-production of its own, non-musical adaption with executive producer Hal B. Wallis at the helm. Wallis was the lifeblood of the studio's top-quality films and liked to be personally involved with his pictures, keeping a close eye on all aspects of production. Known as the "Starmaker," (as the title of his autobiography will attest) Wallis was instrumental in the rise of most of the studio's highly paid talent, including Edward G. Robinson, Bette Davis and in the next decade, Humphrey Bogart.

For the *Robin Hood* project, he hired London-born screenwriter, Rowland Leigh to work up a script treatment with James Cagney as Robin and the studio's stock company as his Merry Men. Wallis also assigned Dr. Herman Lissauer, the studio's research director, and his staff, the gargantuan task of studying 12th century England.

Exactly one month from the date of Dwight Franklin's initial memo, columnist Louella Parsons announced that Cagney had been chosen to play the lead in *The Adventures of Robin Hood* and added that Guy Kibbee (a longtime Warner contract actor) would play Friar Tuck. Within a week, the Hollywood trade paper, *Motion Picture Daily*, was running a full-page ad touting Warners' biggest star in its upcoming spectacle, and production was scheduled to begin when Cagney finished up on his current film project, *The Frisco Kid*.

Relations between Cagney and the studio were rocky, however. Labeled by Jack Warner as the "professional againster," Cagney walked out in November 1935, claiming the studio was overworking him. He sued Warner for breach of contract, when a neighborhood movie theater put costar Pat O'Brien's name above his on the marquee when screening their film, *Ceiling Zero*. His contract stipulated that he would always receive top billing. Research and scriptwriting on *Robin Hood* continued, however, and studio heads came together on a replacement for the disgruntled actor.

Warner Brothers star, James Cagney in
***A Midsummer Night's Dream* (1935)**

At the same time as Cagney's departure from the studio, the pirate adventure, *Captain Blood*, was preparing for release. The film had its own share of casting woes, when the original lead, Robert Donat (yet again) backed out of his contract. English star, Leslie Howard was sought out to play Dr. Peter Blood but wasn't interested, then fellow Brit, Brian Aherne tested for the part. Along with Aherne, there was another young contract player to be given a test. A twenty-six-year-old Tasmanian-born actor named Errol Flynn.

Persuaded in part by Flynn's agent, Minna Wallis (who also happened to be Hal Wallis's sister), Jack Warner took a chance on Errol and gave him the lead in *Captain Blood*. He had already become fascinated by Flynn, who "reminded him of John Barrymore, a hard-drinking, wenching, lovable and handsome man," attributes Warner would have liked for himself. The newcomer experienced a bumpy start, however, on the *Captain Blood* set. Flynn was "amateurish and clumsy with a sword" despite extensive training with fencing instructor, Fred Cavens. He was late and lacked discipline, and fought constantly with the film's director, Michael Curtiz, who had a reputation for being overbearing. Curtiz became easily exasperated with Flynn, and several early scenes had to be reshot to cover the actor's inadequacies, with stuntmen doubling in the duel scenes. Despite all the setbacks, Flynn improved and when the picture was released just after Christmas, 1935, it was a huge success. The new star was immediately cast in another big budget action film called *The Charge of the Light Brigade*, based on Alfred, Lord Tennyson's famed poem. In early February, *Variety* announced that Flynn had been cast as Robin Hood.

With the help of executive story editor, Walter MacEwen, Rowland Leigh continued to work on the script treatment for *Robin Hood*. During the first week of January 1936, Wallis instructed the writers to lay the story out with Flynn in mind. He also sent a message to Jack Warner suggesting the studio "publicize this now and let Cagney know he is losing these properties by his attitude." The rogue star's salary was suspended on December 8 and Cagney – with court approval, while his lawsuit was pending – went on to make two flops for independent studio Grand National Pictures before finally returning to the Warner nest in 1938.

Discussions between MGM and Warners, regarding the respective rights each studio needed for its own *Robin Hood* movie, concluded in May 1936. The agreement allowed Warner the script materials held by Metro which it had acquired from Reliance Pictures. It also gave them the right to make a straight dramatic film without singing, to be released before February 14, 1938. Warner Brothers, in turn, gave MGM all interest in the de Koven operetta version of the tale, with the provision that any potential version be withheld from release until the end of 1939 (With the subsequent success of the Warner film, an MGM musical version never materialized).

In November 1936, Leigh finished his first draft continuity which was then given to studio researcher, Herman Lissauer, his assistant, and a staff of seven historical investigators. The group read the script, made notes based on their research, then checked and returned the document to its authors. To ensure the historical integrity of the dialogue, the notes included reminders and corrections, including the fact that Prince John was never actually regent, that shillings weren't in use until later in history, and that the English didn't become tea drinkers until around 1650. They suggested caution for describing Maid Marian's "boudoir," noting that ladies didn't have boudoirs then, "they had rooms, and none were frilly."

Hal Wallis did not read the completed draft until the following March and was not enthusiastic about it. One point that specifically struck him as a plot weakness was the initial relationship between the story's lovers. In a June 1937 memo to Henry Blanke, who had been assigned as film's associate producer, Wallis said: "The development of the romance between Marian and Robin is too quick. She sees him when he is first brought in and given a beating and then has him freed and the next time she meets him there is a passionate love scene in Sherwood." In fact, in his early notes for the draft, writer Rowland Leigh went so far as to say: "I would strenuously put forth the suggestion in this case either that Maid Marian be omitted completely, in that she is a later... addition to the story of Robin Hood, or that she be brought in as little as possible, because women had no place in the scheme of life of Robin Hood and his band of merry men." Top brass found this suggestion outrageous. Not only was Lady Marian's character expanded in the final version, but a romantic triangle between the character, Robin and Sir Guy of Gisbourne was developed, an idea that originated in the De Koven-Smith light opera and used again in the Fairbanks movie version.

Wallis also complained of "a lot of dull stuff in the script," but the biggest issue was the dialogue, which he thought "too poetical" and "too much like *Midsummer Night's Dream.*" Wrote Wallis:

> "You cannot have the maid or anyone else reading lines such as, 'Oh, Milord, tarry not too long for, I fear, in her remorse, she may fling herself from the window – some harm will befall her, I know!'... it won't do."

Wallis needed a new and better script and in April 1937, he assigned contract writer Norman Reilly Raine to the job of rewriting. Raine had recently collaborated on the screenplay for *The Life of Emile Zola*, for which he would win the Academy Award. He was given the story material acquired from MGM's trade with Warners, as well as the Leigh screen treatment and the studio research data to work with and improve upon. The next month, Walter MacEwen instructed Raine in a memo to "keep color in mind when rewriting the script." The story editor continued, "When we originally started on *Robin Hood* it was not contemplated as a Technicolor production. But now . . . Mr. Warner wants to be sure that every advantage is taken of the color medium." Using the work previously compiled by Leigh and others writing on the Robin Hood theme, Raine completed the first draft of his version by mid-summer. His own approach was clearly evident, but the ideas developed by his predecessors shone through as well.

As a literary figure, Robin Hood was a key character in Sir Walter Scott's *Ivanhoe*, as well as Howard Pyle's prose collection of the legend. Many of the aspects and fictional events from these author's ballads were incorporated into Raine's script. This draft portrayed Sir Robin of Locksley as a Saxon knight, as opposed to the yeoman he was presented as in Leigh's original treatment.

To direct the picture, Wallis assigned William Keighley, one of the studio's solid contract directors. Keighley made his way to Hollywood via Broadway shortly after the advent of sound. He landed a job with Warner Brothers, first as an assistant director, then a dialogue director before receiving his first full directing credit in 1934. Refined and urbane, Keighley affected a British accent during his time as an actor in an English theatrical company, though he was born in Philadelphia. Despite his cultured background he made a name for himself directing the hard-boiled gangster fare that Warners did best, specifically *G-Men* with Cagney and *Bullets or Ballots* with Edward G. Robinson. Keighley was assigned to *Robin Hood* shortly after completing *The Prince and the Pauper*, another classic period piece featuring Flynn, with whom the director got along famously.

On July 6, Wallis informed Blanke that "the budget on Robin Hood according the last script [the Rowland Leigh version] is $1,185,000... Of course, we cannot have a budget of this kind on the picture and on the rewrite let us bear this in mind and work towards the elimination of the huge mob scenes that were called for in the original script." A meeting was arranged between Wallis, Blanke and Keighley to discuss any script changes necessary to tighten the budget. Yet another studio writer, Seton I. Miller, was assigned to collaborate with Raine for more revisions, which Wallis

**Warner Brothers Executive Producer
Hal B. Wallis**

wanted completed by early September. When a working script was finally ready (this time with the dialogue more modern in tone), and with most of the cast assembled, initial filming was in sight.

The Warner Brothers took their budgets to heart. Jack Warner was notorious for money-saving measures, including walks around the studio lot, turning off light switches carelessly left on by others. Coming through the hardscrabble early years, the studio was famous for paring film costs to the bone. "Listen, a picture, all it is is an expensive dream," Harry Warner once told a reporter. "Well, it's just as easy to dream for $700,000 as for $1,500,000."

ERROL AND OLIVIA

**Young Warners' Contract Player,
Errol Flynn**

Errol Flynn was six feet, two inches tall and one hundred and eighty pounds. Broad of both shoulders and chest, he was lean and muscular. An avid outdoorsman, he was bronzed from the sun, and his wicked, rakish smile completed a package of raw sexuality that women could not resist. His longtime friend, actor David Niven, would describe him as "a magnificent specimen of the rampant male." His boss, Jack Warner, used the same word, explaining Flynn's appeal aptly: "He had mediocre talent," he said, "but to the Walter Mittys of the world he was all the heroes in one magnificent, sexy, animal package." His good looks and impish charm combined to make him the perfect romantic hero for Depression-era Hollywood.

He was born in Hobart, Tasmania in 1909 as Errol Leslie Thomson Flynn, though he eventually dropped the Leslie because, as he would later declare, "I had an uncle of that name and we hated each other's guts." He was described by his mother as "a devil in boy's clothing," and his relationship with her was turbulent to say the least. Flynn would later confess that their constant quarrels would bring a time "when it was a matter of indifference to me whether I saw her or not." His mother's people were "seafaring folk," and she had an ancestor named Midshipman Young, who was the chief aide of Fletcher Christian of *Mutiny on the Bounty* and accompanied him to Pitcairn Island.

After a time at a London school, seventeen-year-old Flynn returned to Australia to continue his education at the Sydney Church of England Grammar School. He admitted in his autobiography that he could not "manage the tests and examinations and grades," and that he "was in revolt against all formal schooling." His accomplishments "were strictly physical." He boasted: "I was bigger than most. I was an athlete, quite good at tennis, swimming, boxing, and ready to fight, if picked on." After being expelled from Sydney

Grammar (for either seducing the daughter of the school's laundress or stealing the tennis team's slush fund, or both), his formal education was ended, and he found a job as a mail clerk at Dalgety and Company, a large shipping firm in Sydney. Within a year he was fired for pilfering funds from the department's cash box.

Always out for adventure, Flynn next headed to New Guinea, seeking his fortune after hearing gold was discovered there. The now eighteen-year-old endeavored to become a cadet patrol officer, a program which included two years of intense training and required successful completion of high school examinations (which Flynn did not possess). Errol was given a temporary position until his references from Sydney arrived. What arrived instead were letters from Dalgety's and Company, and the young rogue was again out on his ear.

The next few years were spent running a tobacco plantation, boxing at a local level (he was quite good) and womanizing. Then, in 1932, Flynn met Australian filmmaker Charles Chauvel, who was making a film about the famed mutiny on the *Bounty* incident which occurred in the South Seas during the late sixteenth-century. Flynn was cast in one of the leads as Fletcher Christian. Although the movie was made in two months and had a fleeting running time of sixty-six minutes, it would be famous as the film debut of Errol Flynn. It sparked an interest that would eventually lead to a full-time career. Flynn recounted: "I was startled to note that I could remember the lines I had to say. I could commit lines to memory and not falter.... It was a big discovery in a way."

His "big discovery" led him to England, where he landed a job with the Northampton Repertory Players, playing a wide variety of characters at night while looking for film work during the day. He worked as an extra in a movie called, *I Adore You* in 1933, then met Irving Asher, the managing director of Teddington Studios, the British branch of Warner Brothers. Impressed with his "physical attributes, personality and intelligence," Asher offered Flynn a contract and cabled Warners' Hollywood office in shorthand in October 1934:

> Signed today seven years' optional contract best picture bet we have ever seen. He twenty-five Irish looks cross between Charles Farrell and George Brent same type and build excellent actor champion boxer swimmer guarantee he real find.

The handsome actor was immediately cast as the lead in a "quota quickie" mystery called *Murder at Monte Carlo*, when Jack Warner, brought him to Hollywood for a six-month contract at $150 a week. While on board the ship, *The Paris*, from London to New York, Flynn met French actress Lili Damita. "Everything about her was arrogant," he said, "and the more arrogant the more beautiful." Besides being beautiful, Damita was well-connected and five years his senior. The two married a few months after his arrival in Hollywood.

His American movie debut was inauspicious, to say the least, playing a corpse in yet another mystery, *The Case of the Curious Bride*. Then he appeared in a B-picture called, *Don't Bet on Blondes*, both filmed in 1935. His casting in *Captain Blood* was a game changer, and upon its

Errol Flynn and his first wife, actress Lili Damita

release Flynn became a star. So big, in fact, that Warners redirected his upcoming filming schedule, taking him out as the second lead to Fredric March in the blockbuster-budgeted *Anthony Adverse* and ushering him into the lead role in another action yarn, *The Charge of the Light Brigade*.

As with most actors of the day, publicity departments would spin completely different histories for its stars or at the very least build up or tone down their past (whichever was required). More than one chuckle would be had for those who knew Flynn, regarding an article published by the *Sydney Morning Herald* about the fledgling star's 'quiet' lifestyle. "Girls and hero-worshipping young women were always a source of worry to him," claimed the piece. "for, in spite of his assured manner, he was a retiring type, who asked nothing better than to be left alone with a pipe and a book." To the contrary! His rampant womanizing would continue after marriage to Damita, with whom he had a tumultuous relationship. "We were poles apart, except in bed," he said of his wife. "Mentally, woefully inadequate. Sexually, fabulous, wonderfully exciting, beautiful. All this became the source of an irritation that grew and grew."

Damita may have been Flynn's spouse, but moviegoers in 1936 had taken a liking to Errol's on-screen pairing with a young Warner Brothers contract actress named Oliva de Havilland. The movie couple had risen together with their joint success in both *Captain Blood* and *The Charge of the Light Brigade* (which became Warners' biggest hit of 1936), and by autumn would be cast together again in *Robin Hood*. Irony played a part in de Havilland's success, as she wasn't the first choice in any of these films, and to say that the role of Marian was a boon to her career is an understatement. It was a solid step in a career less than two years running.

Like Errol Flynn, de Havilland was born in a country to the far right of the world map; in Tokyo, on June 1, 1916. The following year her only sibling, Joan (later Fontaine) would be born there as well. Their parents' marriage was "doomed from the start," and headed for divorce court after Mrs. de Havilland discovered her husband was unfaithful with the household's Japanese maid. (Mr. de Havilland would later marry his *geisha*) Due to both daughters' poor

Flynn and Olivia de Havilland in a publicity photo for
Captain Blood (1935)

health, Lillian de Havilland took them to the United States, settling in Saratoga, California.

As a teenager, Olivia became interested in school dramatics and branched out into local theater groups. In 1934, after graduating high school, she was offered the role of Puck in *A Midsummer Night's Dream* at the Saratoga Community Theater. An assistant of producer Max Reinhardt saw Olivia in the play and offered her the part of understudy to Hermia in Reinhardt's famed production of the same story at the Hollywood Bowl. When Warner Brothers wanted to make a motion picture version the following year, de Havilland was asked to join the cast and was placed under a long-term contract with the studio. Upon his first meeting with the young actress, Jack Warner noted: "I saw a girl with big, soft brown eyes... a fresh young beauty that would soon stir a lot of tired old muscles around the film town." It was a grand film debut for the still teenaged performer, though she was placed in some routine programmers before being cast in *Captain Blood*.

Studio contract player Jean Muir was the original pick for the female lead in *Blood*, chosen as a complement for Robert Donat, but when the actor backed out, Warner Brothers replaced her. Pretty blonde Warners' actress Anita Louise was mentioned as the romantic lead in *Light Brigade* as late as March 1936, but less than two weeks later *Variety* reported that de Havilland had the part. In fact, a late March memo from Jack Warner to producer Wallis acknowledged "we must insist on using de Havilland," while assuring the decision was "in no way any reflection on Anita Louise, whom we all admire." Louise was eventually paired with Flynn in the 1937 drama, *Green Light*, but only when Olivia was assigned another project.

As casting time for Lady Marian approached, Louise was under serious consideration by Jack Warner, because she wasn't currently assigned to a picture and Warner hated for any contract player to be idle while still being paid. Hal Wallis preferred de Havilland, however, due to the proven screen success she offered with Flynn in their two previous films together. With Wallis's backing it was announced in mid-September that she was cast in the role. The producer gave strict instructions, however, that public notification of the choice be withheld until Louise had been informed directly. The decision caused a reported "bitter feud" between the actresses, who never met on a soundstage, though they appeared in three movies together: *Anthony Adverse, Call it a Day* and *A Midsummer Night's Dream*. Said one newspaper, "Miss Louise recently was reported to have protested to Warner Brothers executives because Miss de Havilland was finally chosen to play roles for which she was originally considered." Anita Louise would remain under contract to Warner Brothers until 1938, after which she worked as a freelance actress.

The chemistry between Flynn and de Havilland was genuine. From their time on the set of *Captain Blood* there were sparks enough between them for boss Jack Warner to observe: "Together these two amateurs set the screen on fire." When Jean Muir tested with Flynn for *Blood*, he would stare at her forehead instead of into her eyes, which threw her off and caused her to miss her lines. He did not use the same approach when testing with Olivia. "During the making of *Captain Blood* I had grown very fond of Olivia de Havilland," he recalled in his memoirs. "By the time we made *The Charge of the Light Brigade* I was sure I was in love with her." She, in turn, was captivated from their first meeting.

As for the rest of the cast, the vision of Dwight Franklin in his original memo to Jack Warner never reached fruition, but the basic idea of high-profile Warner Brothers character actors becoming the residents of Sherwood Forest did come to pass. There was much villainy in the completed script and filling these roles of dastardly degenerates were some of Hollywood's most skilled and best-known screen heavies. Claude Rains was cast as the tyrannical Saxon oppressor, Prince John, the first of four roles under his newly signed one-year contract with Warners, and Basil Rathbone was hired as his haughty henchman, Sir Guy of Gisborne.

Rains made his Hollywood film debut four years earlier in the Universal horror classic, *The Invisible Man*.

Suave villain Basil Rathbone as Sir Guy of Gisbourne

After plans to cast Boris Karloff and Colin Clive for that role fell through, Rains was chosen by the film's director, James Whale, who thought his "soothing voice" would be a great contrast to the violent nature of his character. When slated to play Prince John, Rains wasn't sure how to approach the part, but when he learned that he would be wearing a rust-colored, heavily banged pageboy bob, he confided in his daughter that "all the henna, ermine and brocade" inspired him to play the prince as "tacitly homosexual." Actor Roddy McDowell always believed that Rains' performance was based on the "stylized voice and mannerisms" of Warners' contract actress, Bette Davis. When McDowell confessed his idea to Rains years later, Rains merely answered with an "enigmatic smile."

As the menacing Sir Guy, Basil Rathbone displayed the sardonic sneer that earned him the reputation as one of Hollywood's strongest villains, as well as a minimum of $2,000 a week as a freelance performer. (Reports listed the amount as high as $6,000 by April 1938). Born in Johannesburg, South Africa and raised in England, Rathbone was trained as a Shakespearean actor. His theatrical career was interrupted during World War I, when he served as an intelligence officer, later being awarded the Military Cross. He came to the United States to act on the New York stage, eventually making his way to Hollywood and gaining a reputation playing sinister rogues in top drawer productions like MGM's *David Copperfield* and *Anna Karenina*. He and Flynn appeared together in *Captain Blood* (with Rathbone again playing the villain), with the actors displaying their swordplay skills in a rousing and dramatic duel. Rathbone enjoyed fencing immensely and practiced regularly. In his memoir, he assessed his relationship with Flynn, both as a co-star and acquaintance:

> "He was monstrously lazy and self-indulgent, relying on a magnificent body to keep him going, and he had an insidious flair for making trouble, mostly for himself. I believe him to have been quite fearless, and subconsciously possessed of his own self-destruction. I would say that he was fond of me, for what reason I shall never know. It was always 'dear old Bazzz,' and he would flash that smile that was both defiant and cruel, but which for me always had a tinge of affection in it. We only crossed swords, never words, and he was generous and appreciative of my work. I like him and he liked me."

Popular British actor, David Niven was initially chosen to play Robin's chief chum in Sherwood, Will Scarlet, but when he was unavailable, the role was given to Patric Knowles, whom Flynn had met at Warners' Teddington Studios in England. Tall, handsome and very British, Knowles was brought to Hollywood by the studio in 1936 as a threat to their rapidly rising, frequently misbehaving star, whom Knowles resembled. The studio cast him as Flynn's brother in *The Charge of the Light Brigade* and instead of becoming rivals, the two men became great chums, with Knowles described as "Flynn's boon companion in debauchery." The actors became so close that Flynn was named godfather to Knowles' son.

Distinguished and patrician looking Ian Hunter was cast as King Richard the Lionheart. Like Rathbone, Hunter was born in South Africa and served in World War I. He started in pictures in the mid-1920s, first in Britain then America, settling in at Warner Brothers by the time *Robin Hood* began production. Other studio stalwarts assigned to the film were Melville Cooper as the cowardly, bumbling High Sheriff of Nottingham and Alan Hale as Little John. A failed opera singer, Hale was a burly, wavy-haired character actor who found his niche playing loveable buffoons and boisterous sidekicks. Being cast as Little John was a case of déjà vu, as he played the part in the 1922 Doug Fairbanks version, and he would play it yet again, albeit an older, less vigorous version, in 1950's *Rogues of Sherwood Forest* at Columbia.

Although Guy Kibbee was originally announced for the Friar Tuck role in 1935, he was no longer under contract to Warner Brothers, and Eugene Pallette, a freelance performer, was chosen instead. Pallette was immediately recognizable to Depression-era moviegoers by his huge girth and gravelly bark of a voice. He excelled in screwball comedies of the period (most notably *My Man Godfrey*) and brought his blustery, irascible screen persona to the role of the rotund friar. With the production date close at hand, Una O'Connor was assigned the role of Bess, maid servant to Lady Marian. Her thick Irish brogue and pop-eyed look of fear or outrage made her a memorable addition to the horror classics, *The Invisible Man* (1933) and *Bride of Frankenstein* (1935). Like Pallette and Alan Hale, she was used as comic relief among the throng of characters in *Robin Hood*.

With casting complete, and a working script in place, it was time to begin. Cast and crew headed north to Chico,

California where location shooting would begin in late September. Amidst the huge trees of Chico would be created the perfect Sherwood Forest of Merry Olde England. It was one of the most ambitious and expensive undertakings by the film community at any studio and it would be fraught with challenges and problems at every corner.

WELCOME TO SHERWOOD!

Flynn and de Havilland with director William Keighley on location in Chico, California

Chico, in northern California, was a town of eight thousand people in 1937. Its city limits spread several miles into the foothills of the Sierra Nevada mountains and in 1905, a large tract of land was donated by the widow of the city's founder, John Bidwell, creating Bidwell Park. It was the perfect location to recreate the medieval stomping grounds of the legendary archer, a majestic 2,400-acre woodland that ran up into the jagged Chico canyon along

Big Chico Creek. The forest of Bidwell Park was adorned throughout with giant sycamores and massive, sturdy oaks, some draped with vines. There was some initial concern, however, about the location choice with the rainy season approaching in early October.

Production manager, Tenney Wright sent a memo to Hal Wallis questioning: "I wonder if we are wrong in allowing Robin Hood to be shot in Chico?... If it rains one day, it will take another day to dry out, particularly in the woods, under the trees." He was also concerned with the "burden" of transportation costs for cast, crew and equipment. The decision was made, however, and a special ten-car train carried over 300 people, including extras, make-up artists, technicians, electricians, stunt men and various other movie personnel, 450 miles north of Hollywood to the Bidwell Park location. Also, in tow were fifty horses in the baggage cars, a squirrel, an owl and a trained deer. One report estimated that in addition, a fleet of forty trucks would be needed to transport the production unit.

The starting budget for the film was $1,600,000, and of this amount, over $100,000 was for props alone. More than 20,000 items were listed among the props used – including some 10,000 arrows – all of which were made by a massive studio staff. Other items of manufactured medievalry included quarter staffs, maces, war flails, battle axes, neck and leg chains, period bread boards, baking sticks, 12th century trumpets and musical instruments, arm guards, armor for men and horses, money, lamps, drinking vessels, cooking utensils, long bows, cross bows, quivers, lances, pennants, broad swords and scores of other items, created from information found in rare and valuable old books pertaining to the period. The studio was able to save the manpower of producing soldier's and knight's saddles thanks to Cecil B. DeMille, who already had them made for his epic, *The Crusades*, two years earlier and Warners simply rented them from the Western Costume Company. Since planned filming would continue at the location for six weeks, the caravan would also include everything that would make the company self-sufficient for that time. Tons of foodstuffs, medical supplies, personal baggage and mechanical equipment found its way onto the great fleet.

Key technical staff arrived on September 15 to prepare and set up the location. In addition to Keighley and a handful of others, the staff consisted of Park Frame, location manager, and Al Alborn, unit manager. Art director Carl Jules Weyl had the park's foliage supplemented with hundreds of bushes, ferns and flowers, as well as artificial greenery. In addition, steel reinforced artificial trees were installed for the forest acrobatics to be demonstrated by the medieval merry men – a request made by Chico's city fathers, fearful that Bidwell's giant trees might be harmed during filming. With autumn nearly upon the area, vegetable dye was sprayed on the changing leaves to give the appearance of a lush, green English forest. Large tents were set up near the gates of the Lower Park, the portion of Bidwell being used for filming. "Warner City," as it was known, housed make-up artists, hairdressers and costumers, as well as a field hospital for any potential injuries. Stables were built for horses and kennels set up for domestic and hunting dogs.

Flynn ended a four-week vacation on August 12 and was scheduled for costume and preliminary tests at the studio. Attempting to stave off any problems with the film's star before they began, production manager Tenney Wright wrote Jack Warner: "Kindly have a talk with Mr. Flynn and tell him to be on time for his call .... Also, he is not to be dissipating around and come into the studio with bags under his eyes, as this is a very expensive picture .... Get him straightened out before we go into production." Flynn and others cast members were housed in the hotel at the Richardson Springs Resort in the mountains just north of Chico. With filming taking many weeks, the cast and crew were eagerly recognized as part of the local community, albeit a temporary addition. Employees at the Richardson Springs hotel knew all the stars on a first name basis and the crew would watch movies on the outdoor screen, play shuffleboard and have dances in the ballroom. When an eleven-year-old female fan met Flynn, he kissed her hand, which she claimed not to have washed for a week. She later, however, blushingly admitted to preferring his less flamboyant co-star, Patric Knowles.

Shooting finally began on Monday, September 27, 1937. The first scene to be filmed by Keighley would be shot along the banks of the Big Chico Creek, the quarterstaff battle and first meeting of Robin and Little John. It was both intense and humorous and would be the second of thirteen films that Flynn and Alan Hale would make together at Warner Brothers, establishing a "buddy" camaraderie that lasted a decade. Flynn fondly remembered working with Hale: "He was such a good actor

Flynn with buddy, Patric Knowles between takes on the Robin Hood set in Chico

that if he was with you in a scene he could take it away from you, whether he was standing behind you, beside you, or in front of you… Luckily for me, he liked me, so he never pulled any of his scene-stealing with me." As Keighley painstakingly set up the shot, a heavy fog rolled in from the coast, halting filming. The sequence was again prepared at great length the next morning and the next with the same frustrating and costly result. The director's "passion for unnecessary detail" combined with weather delays weren't making for happy executives back home at the Burbank headquarters. "At the rate of three days to shoot one little sequence," wrote Wallis to Keighley, "we have cause for worry."

Three days after initial filming began, a similar scene between Flynn and Eugene Pallette as Friar Tuck posed its own challenges. Again, the scene took place alongside, as well as in Chico Creek. The ideal location was chosen for a broadsword duel in midstream between Robin and the portly Friar when noisy rapids a few yards away made it impossible for the sound engineers to properly record the dialogue between the actors. With the help of several of the grips a "creek silencer" was developed with long strips of heavy sacking, which were weighted down and completely covered the fifteen yards of rocks which were causing the small series of rapids. With the noise down to a murmur, recording was able to resume.

According to several versions of the legend, the first meeting of Tuck and Robin culminated in a battle of wits in which each respectively gained the upper hand and forced the other to carry him across the creek. While rehearsing the part of the scene where Robin carried the fat Friar "piggy-back," a double was used for Flynn. Pallette's 280 pounds proved too much for the stand-in and the rotund actor fell, fracturing a small bone in his left wrist. In the final film the back-and-forth across the creek was edited to just one time, with Flynn being the one hauled into the water. (As the duo is making their way into the water in the final print, the damp bottoms of their costumes can be viewed as evidence of the earlier filming).

As the company settled into work at Bidwell and shooting began, huge crowds of fans and onlookers poured into the park, excited and intrigued to watch the filming. City authorities could not block off any section of the park due to a stipulation from its founder that no member of the public should be denied access. They did, however, launch a campaign in local newspapers, pleading with residents to stay out of camera range and keep as quiet as possible. The requests proved successful. Director Keighley observed: "One Sunday there were thousands in the park, most of them watching the set, but not a single take was ruined by noise or by anyone getting within camera range. We had a loud-speaker system, of course, which helped immensely in controlling the crowds." The excitement extended outside the boundaries of Bidwell Park as well. As the citizenry went "movie mad," Chico enjoyed a small-sized boom, with stores doing record business and hotels and restaurants at capacity. 103 local men were also hired as extras for the scenes set at Robin's woodland camp, boosting the local economy even further.

If residents of the northern California community were happy with the production, those involved with it back in Hollywood were less than thrilled. The week before initial filming began in Chico, Hal Wallis held a meeting with associate producer Henry Blanke, script writer Norman Reilly Raine, studio production manager Tenney Wright and Keighley to discuss the movie's budget. There was strong disagreement about a huge, expensive jousting tournament scene that Keighley argued was the "big production splash" necessary at the beginning of the picture. He believed that people who remembered the 1922 Fairbanks version would expect "something spectacular," and that it set the tone of the "pageantry of the period."

Raine felt Keighley's ideas were "sincere but misguided," explaining in a memo to Wallis that people did not remember the details of the Fairbanks film and that the pageantry would be found in the script and the background scenery, especially since it would be filmed in Technicolor.

The writer added that Keighley's overly-ambitious vision would put the climax of the picture at the beginning with the only way to top it to have "a slam-bang hell of a battle or something equally spectacular – and expensive – at the end." Raine's interpretation was to focus the story on Robin Hood, "the swashbuckling, reckless, rakehell type of character," instead of knights, castles and tournaments that surrounded his character. He argued that the pomp and splendor of the archery tournament, a key scene in the film, would "certainly suffer pictorially" if a jousting tournament was tacked on as a prelude. Observed Raine: "Christ's second coming in a cloud of glory would seem tame if we showed the creation of the world first." Within two weeks the jousting tournament was out.

The reference to color was important, because the crayon laden hues of Technicolor played an equally important part in the movie as the talent laden skills of its cast. The trademarked Technicolor process had been around since 1916, and hand-tinted color was used before that. It wasn't until the 1930s, however, with the advent of the three-strip Technicolor system that the process made a permanent impact. In 1935, *Becky Sharp* became the first feature film entirely photographed in the three-strip system, ushering in a slow, but steady use of Technicolor in Hollywood. The producer of *Becky Sharp*, Kenneth

Macgowan, had this forewarning to glamour girls about the new process:

> "Ungentlemanly Technicolor definitely prefers brunettes. They are easier to print. Shadows, dark colors always come out best. Thin, subtle, palid [sic] shades make tremendous demands on the new art. Natural blondes, like Ann Harding survive this acid test magnificently. Miriam Hopkins [the film's star] never looked so beautiful as in *Becky Sharp*. But let platinums beware! And as for these lovely ladies who have molded strange new personalities out of black-gashed mouths, Arc-de-Triomphe eyebrows and antennae eyelashes – black and white caricatures from some aphrodisian inferno – what they are going to look like in color I haven't the faintest idea. Except that you won't be able to recognize them without a guide book."

With the success of *Becky Sharp*, five more films went into production using the process in 1936. *Ramona* at 20th Century-Fox; *The Trail of the Lonesome Pine* at Paramount; *Dancing Pirate* at RKO; *The Garden of Allah* at Selznick International and *God's Country and the Woman* at Warner Brothers. Both *God's Country* and Warners' next color feature, *Gold is Where You Find It*, an outdoor drama set in late 19th century California, proved to be an inauspicious debut of the format for the studio. *Variety* held little hope for the success of *God's Country and the Woman*, saying the "fact that it was made in Technicolor adds little to its box office chances," and of *Gold is Where You Find It*, *Film Bulletin* claimed there was "too much emphasis on the pictorial beauty of its Technicolor finery."

Still, both pictures did respectable business and set the momentum for a third, larger scale production.

When the first script treatment of *Robin Hood* proved unsatisfactory, Walter MacEwen instructed screenwriter Norman Reilly Raine to "keep color in mind when rewriting the script." The story editor explained: "When we originally started on *Robin Hood* it was not contemplated as a Technicolor production. But now... Mr. Warner wants to be sure that every advantage is taken of the color medium."

The film's cinematographer, Tony Gaudio, came with strong bona fides, having won an Academy Award for his work on *Anthony Adverse* the previous year, as well as shooting *God's Country and the Woman*, which was directed by Keighley. Motion picture companies didn't own the Technicolor system or its cameras, they rented them, along with the services of special technicians and supervisors. Large, bulky and cumbersome, there were only eleven of the specialized cameras in existence when *Robin Hood* was filmed, and that production used them all. The expense was massive, and with no completed script, Warner Brothers had to postpone its commitment for use of the cameras and equipment from the end of August until later in September.

Research director Herman Lissauer and his staff continued their work to ensure historical integrity and accuracy. For the art department it consulted old books and prints showing medieval castles, apartments, streets and dwellings. For the costumes it excavated authentic notes on what milady wore to an archery tournament, to court, to market, to sleep and the equivalents for male aristocracy. On games and customs, staff members spent Sundays reading at least thirty sources on Saxon pleasures and Norman fads, gathering information to relay to Keighley. The research stopped the use of silk pennants for the archery tournament. Silks were too rare and expensive to allow this custom.

The research and making of costumes took many months, as period detail had to coordinate with Technicolor design. Undertaking the massive task was Warner Brothers' costume designer, Milo Anderson. Only twenty-seven years old when *Robin Hood* was produced, Anderson became a top costumer in Hollywood at an extremely early age. He realized his interest in costume design as a freshman in high school while taking a class on set design. Instead of enrolling in the costume design class, which was considered a class for girls, Anderson began an independent study of the art in his off time. His high school boyfriend caught the eye of MGM designer, Adrian, but the young man preferred Anderson. When producer Samuel Goldwyn needed someone to replace Coco Chanel as costume designer for his film, *The Greeks Had a Word for Them*, he tried to borrow couture master Adrian from Metro. The studio refused to loan out their top designer and Adrian sarcastically suggested Anderson be given the job, bitter over his scorned love interest. The joke ended up being on Adrian when Goldwyn took his recommendation and hired Anderson, whose sketches were a success. He worked briefly for Goldwyn before moving over to Warner Brothers in 1933. According to film historian and costumer, David

Chierichetti, "Milo knew what worked, what caught the eye, and from his youth was never afraid to say so."

For *Robin Hood*, Anderson was faced with wardrobe challenges. One specific instance involved a knight's armor. After chain mesh armor was made for various knights and soldiers, the sound technicians discovered that the noise of the chain mesh in action was extremely loud. Anderson finally devised a realistic-looking substitute out of woven string, sprayed with metal paint. The final tally saw a costuming bill of $450,000 under Milo Anderson's watch, an estimated $10,000 of which was spent on de Havilland's costumes alone.

Anderson, Technicolor, an extremely fine cast, as well as a highly skilled research team, all contributed to the huge undertaking that was becoming *The Adventures of Robin Hood*. Progress was being made but not fast enough. The budget on the film, already exorbitant, was rapidly growing by the week. And then there was Flynn, the charismatic, athletic fireball with a lust for all that life offered. Surely, no one expected him to just sit and twiddle his thumbs.

ROBIN AT PLAY

**De Havilland and Rathbone taking a
break on the Robin Hood set**

As pre-production commenced, it became clear that a movie about Robin Hood would require a more than adequate knowledge of archery. Bows and arrows were the name of the game and a squad of actors and extras who looked weak with these implements would be not only unacceptable, but impossible. An audition was organized to find a suitable candidate to train and instruct cast members in the handling of bows and arrows. A forty-yard archery range was set up on Stage One and fifty archers were chosen from the numerous competitors who showed up in hopes of a job. Elimination reduced the group from fifty to five and they were then told to shoot in rapid succession the arrows that had been provided. Out of thirteen arrows, one man shot nine bullseyes and four sevens—which is the second circle just outside the bullseye. His name was Howard Hill and he got the job. "You're hired," Keighley said. "Tell the head property man what equipment you want and report Monday to teach twenty-two stock actors and six principals how to shoot."

Hill was a real-life Robin Hood. He didn't rob from the rich to give to the poor (not that any Hollywood columnist reported anyway) and he didn't gallop around the English countryside in a green jerkin. He was, however, reported to have killed with his bow and arrow a 1400-lb. buffalo and a Rocky Mountain big horn sheep. The skilled marksman also "put four arrows into the charging bulk of an 800 lb. black bear, with fatal results," and claimed panthers, wolves and alligators among his prey. Also, a wonderful trick shot, he could knock an apple off a man's head, shoot cigarettes out of the mouths of steady-nerved people, and was adept at shooting fish.

Thirty-seven-year-old Hill hailed from rural Alabama. Tall and powerfully built (6' 2" and 200 lbs.), he excelled in athletics, playing football, baseball and basketball at Auburn Polytechnic Institute (now Auburn University). In the 1920s, while working a fulltime job, Hill played semi-pro baseball on the side and worked as a golf pro on the weekends, but his true passion was archery. No stranger to the screen, he wrote and starred in an outdoor documentary called *The Last Wilderness* in 1935. Howard's amazing archery skills were showcased in a photographic record of large game animals in the American wild. After its release, he rigorously promoted the three-reel short by making personal appearances at each showing, mesmerizing his audiences during intermissions with demonstrations of pinpoint accuracy.

The record-setting champion not only trained and advised the actors on the Robin Hood set, but also donned a costume and made complicated and dangerous trick shots in the film. He was paid $100 a week for twenty-one weeks with a bonus of $100 per complex shot. Ruggedly handsome with thick, dark hair and a moustache, he strongly resembled Flynn and with their mutual interest in hunting and outdoor activities, the two men formed a "long and enduring friendship." In later life, Flynn would proclaim that "some of the truly wonderful moments of my life have been spent tagging along at Howard's heels on our hunting trips in many strange corners of the world."

Hill spent numerous hours teaching Flynn all aspects of archery: proper stance, drawing an arrow from a back quiver, nocking an arrow correctly onto the bowstring, drawing of the bow, aiming and releasing and anything else he might need to know as Robin Hood. Howard wanted Flynn to be at his best, not only for the film's sake, but to protect his reputation as a master archer. To get practice out in the field and have some fun at the same time, the duo sailed to Catalina, dropping anchor at Cherry Cove, a popular mooring on the east side of the island. From there they would paddle a dingy onto shore, then climb the steep bluffs where Flynn could practice his learned skills, hunting wild boar and wild goats. After months of continued, diligent practice, Hill made the last session a long and difficult one, pressuring Flynn to be perfect in each step. Once the lesson was finished, Errol looked at his teacher and said, "You know Howard, there is only one thing that keeps me from hitting you right in the nose." Hill looked back and asked, "What's that?" to which Flynn answered, "FEAR!"

Within two weeks of being on location at Bidwell Park, Flynn fell into trouble while using his newly honed archery skills. He, Hill and a Chico resident, Dave Sanderson, were arrested by a local game warden for possessing pheasants in violation of game laws. Park Frame, Warner Brothers' location manager, posted the $25 bail to the Justice of the Peace for all three men, and the studio's publicity office issued a statement that he'd "shot the pheasants with arrows," as part of his *Robin Hood* training.

Three days later, Flynn was at it again. He and Hill with dogs in tow, went on a Sunday hunting trip in a large wooded area near Richardson Springs. Always competitive and eager to excel in athletic endeavors, the star had become quite expert with his bow and arrow. While hunting, Errol's dog flushed a desert wildcat out of the brush and chased it up a tree. Flynn asked for the first shot, then proceeded to shoot a steel-barbed arrow which entered the bobcat's chest and exited out its back. The shock of the arrow, propelled by a 69-pound bow, knocked the animal several feet into the air before it fell to the ground dead. Unlike the pheasant

Flynn being trained by expert archer, Howard Hill

incident, Flynn was a hero to local farmers, whose young sheep and small farm animals fell prey to the wildcats. Later reports acknowledged that it was Howard who actually killed the cat, letting the star take the credit. Basil Rathbone also accompanied Hill on a bow and arrow excursion, one which ended with Rathbone behind the lens of his 16-millimeter camera (an item he frequently used on his film sets) and Howard standing over his latest conquest: the carcass of a wild boar.

Hill wasn't the only one to share Flynn's company in masculine pursuits during down time in Chico. Fast friends since their time filming *Charge of the Light Brigade*, Errol and Patric Knowles enjoyed a close and jovial camaraderie, and Knowles would remember his high-profile peer with great fondness in later years.

> "Errol Flynn was my friend," said Knowles. "I liked him immensely; in fact, you may substitute the word 'loved' for liked. We have liked thousands of people during our lives. There was only one Errol – a man's man. I was his close companion for many years... I always felt so alive around Flynn. Every moment was used up in an exciting manner; never a dull moment... The 'public Flynn,' or perhaps I should say the Flynn in public, reminded me of a puppy – an overgrown, extremely healthy puppy, who, after being cooped up in a fenced in kennel yard, happily discovers a hole in the fence and makes his escape. The world he discovered outside was so exciting he could hardly stand the ecstasy."

Knowles had recently developed an interest in flying and after filming ended for the day, he and Errol began a habit of regular visits to the small local airfield outside Chico. The owner, Bill Miller, had become friendly with the actors. His operation was small and struggling, boasting only two planes: a Piper Cub and an old Curtis Robin. Knowles had clocked fifty hours of solo flying time as a student, completing a course in Burbank. Flynn had none, but Patric encouraged him to learn to fly the Cub, a skill Flynn picked up immediately. "He lived life as if it were a game – a game he enjoyed playing," recalled Knowles. "But he was an impatient player – not to win, but to move along to the next bout."

The duo began to receive scathing telegrams from the studio after their nightly air antics had been discovered. Warners' warned them of "grave consequences" should anything happen to them while flying. Knowles humorously noted one specific message he received asking, "if I realized that I was endangering the life of the star of the picture and jeopardizing the investment of several million dollars. No one said anything about my life." Ignoring this and other messages, the two continued their evening flights until Knowles received a telegram from Hal Wallis threatening him with legal action if he "persisted in encouraging Flynn to fly." In line with his devil-may-care attitude, Errol told his friend to "tear up the telegram and forget about it." He then suggested they have the driver of the car park it in the hanger so the "snoopers" wouldn't know they were there. They did just that and used the flight to show off, climbing 1,000 feet and performing two loops, making tight turns and wing overs. When they landed, two men were approaching them. One was Park Frame, the Warners' location manager who posted Flynn's bail in the pheasant incident. The other man was a stranger to them. Knowles recalled:

> "The stranger was a Civil Aeronautics Authority man. They had arrived on the field just as I took off and had witnessed my performance. The studio manager informed me that they were going to lodge a complaint with the Screen Actors Guild. The C.A.A. man took away my license pending the outcome of the hearing on my case at a later date. The charges? Flying in a manner to endanger the lives and property of the public. Stunting without a parachute."

> "Later in the car, on the way to our hotel, I asked Flynn where he was during the excitement. 'Why, in the car having forty winks, old son,' he said. 'I started to learn my lines for tomorrow and simply dozed off.'"

The Screen Actors Guild fined Knowles $100 and his license was reinstated at the hearing by the C.A.A.

Amidst all the off-camera fraternity hijinks, Errol's wife, Lili, joined him in Chico. She arrived in early October with eight large trunks filled with luxurious bed sheets and comforters, determined to make her husband's hotel room at Richardson Springs "real cute." Jealousy and suspicion drew her to Northern California, a fact which wasn't lost on gossip columnist Sheila Graham. "Lili Damita is taking no chances with Hubby [sic] Errol Flynn," Graham wrote, "and has joined him at the Chico 'Robin Hood' location." Upon her arrival she wrapped herself around Flynn in a "boa constrictor-like embrace" and posed for publicity shots with her husband dressed as Robin Hood. Errol felt smothered and desperate, saying:

> "Lili was so violently jealous that I suppose she loved me. With my wandering eye, I did nothing to help her overcome her fits of possessiveness... I felt trapped, even asphyxiated by her possessiveness. I had to get away from her. Her bedroom art and her good cooking were not enough. All around me the whole world beckoned."

Damita knew there was chemistry, both on-screen and off, between Flynn and Olivia de Havilland. All of

Hollywood knew it! As early as May 1937, gossip columns were predicting an off-screen pairing of the two actors. One reporter wrote: "If Errol Flynn and Lili Damita finally divorce, as we surmise they will, we'll venture a prophecy. The new Mrs. Flynn will be Olivia de Havilland." When Lili got to Chico, de Havilland wasn't even on set yet. Scenes were being shot around her, as she was still filming *Gold is Where You Find It* in Weaverville, California. When shooting on that picture was completed in mid-October, she made her way to Bidwell Park to begin work on Robin Hood. She arrived in Chico, aboard the Southern Pacific, and avoided a mob at the station by debarking hundreds of yards down the track, where location manager Al Alleborn, two publicists, and fellow cast member Patric Knowles, greeted and escorted her to her hotel.

She was installed in the Hotel Oaks, a stately six-story hostelry in downtown Chico, far removed from Richardson Springs, where Flynn and Damita were staying. It was the first time the actress wasn't accompanied by her mother, Lillian, on location, as she had just turned twenty-one. Instead, she shared her room with her stand-in, Ann Robinson. Initially hired by Warner Brothers at $5 a day, Robinson worked first as a stand-in for Ann Dvorak, then Kay Francis and Margaret Lindsay before finally becoming the permanent double for de Havilland in 1935. By the time she accompanied Olivia to Chico in late 1937, her salary had increased to $50 a week. The two women were friends and de Havilland would act as bridesmaid in Robinson's wedding the following summer.

Flynn's wife, Lili Damita visiting on set in Chico, California

Olivia was still enamored by Flynn while on set, but Lili's presence dampened her ardor. Despite Damita's jealousy and rumors around Hollywood of an affair between the stars, de Havilland was adamant that such a relationship did not exist. "Yes, we did fall in love and I believe that this is evident in the screen chemistry between us," she recounted in later life. "But his circumstances at the time [Damita] prevented the relationship going further… I have not talked about it a great deal but the relationship was not consummated. Chemistry was there though. It was there." She reaffirmed her feelings at the time, saying, "I didn't reject him. You know, I was also very attracted to him. But I said that nothing could happen while he was still with Lili… I said that he had to resolve things with Lili first. But, you know, he never did. I think he was in deep thrall to her in some way. He did not leave her then and he never approached me in that way again. So nothing did ever happen between us."

Still, she was frustrated with Flynn's attempt to seduce her, claiming that his marriage was over, while Lili's presence proved that to be untrue. She sought a little playful revenge. "I thought, well I'm going to torture Errol Flynn," Olivia recalled. "And so we had one kissing scene, [when Robin climbs the castle wall to her chamber] which I looked forward to with great delight. I remember I blew every take. At least six, maybe seven, maybe eight, and we had to kiss all over again. And Errol Flynn got really rather uncomfortable, and he had, if I may say so, a little trouble with his tights."

Workdays were busy and early for de Havilland while on location. Every morning at 5 a.m., she would leave the quaint comforts of the Hotel Oaks and make her way to the enormous tents at Bidwell Park, which housed the hairdressing and makeup departments. She would then be costumed in the Milo Anderson designed gowns before reaching the set. A week after her arrival, an influenza outbreak hit the company, affecting Alan Hale, Patric Knowles and other cast members. Olivia was not spared, and the on-site doctor said she would not be able to work until early the following week. It wasn't the first time the group was threatened with a widespread health issue. Early in production, poison oak was so prevalent at the location that the studio asked the entire company to be inoculated against the vine. A few resisted but followed suit when Flynn volunteered to take the first shot.

During the last week of October, Errol wrote to Hal Wallis complaining of the wig he wore as part of his costume. "I loathe the bloody thing," he said. "With the hat on it's fine, and the alteration I want to suggest does not affect any of the stuff we've shot so far." His "squawk" was the middle part of the wig with fringes of hair falling on his forehead. His proposed alteration would include an unnoticeable part on either side with the fringes swept back off his forehead. The actor reiterated his distaste for the hairpiece, saying: "I hate this present one so much I shudder every time I see the Goddam [sic] thing..." The new wig suggested by Flynn was eventually used in all scenes shot without his hat. In the same memo the actor disclosed his weariness of the location shoot. "I feel like one of the oldest inhabitants of Chico now – we all do. And we're all very sick of it but consoling ourselves with the report or rather rumour that you like the stuff down there. Is it so?"

It was not exactly so. Wallis wasn't happy with much of Keighley's work. On November 1, he wrote the director regarding de Havilland's performance so far: "She seems to have gone elegant on us and her reading of lines is reminiscent of the leading lady in high school plays." More importantly, the executives in Burbank were not pleased at all with the pace of the film. Even sending a second-unit director, B. Reeves "Breezy" Eason, to help speed things along didn't help. The production was over budget and nine days behind schedule. Something had to be done.

TROUBLE AT THE HELM

Flynn sporting his *Robin Hood* costume in the Warner Brothers' commissary with contract actress Gloria Blondell (sister of Joan)

By the first week of November filming at Bidwell Park was done. Posters went up around town advertising a "Farewell Dance" to be held at the Chico High School gymnasium. The local newspaper, the *Chico Enterprise*, reported that on Friday, November 5, the special dance, organized and sponsored by the city's chamber of commerce, would bid goodbye to the Warner Brothers' troupe. It was open not only to the cast members and crew, but the Chico community in general, with enough space to "accommodate about 1,000 couples." Cost $1.00 – Ladies Free.

As part of a publicity campaign launched shortly after leaving Chico, the filming company published a paper, the *Sherwood Forest Gazette*, and printed it on wood parchment. Carrying the dateline of November 11, 1937, Sherwood, England, it featured news, a reader's forum, a column and ads, and used an Olde English typeface. The lead story read: "Ground was broken last week for Sir Guy of Gisborne's new Sherwood castle, located near Nottingham-on-the-Warner. It will be the last word in castles. The dungeons will be deeper and darker than any other in England. The main gates will be guarded by pots of boiling oil and the outer windows will be 80 feet above ground." It also included related classified ads: "Castles to let. Sherwood Realters, Inc. Today's Special: 142 room castlette, 16-foot moat, almost new outdoor plumbing, two torture chambers, burglar proof beds, a bargain at 5200 pounds." In reality, a massive construction effort was being erected on Sound Stage #2 at Warners' Burbank studios. The reimagined Nottingham Castle would occupy the entire length and breadth of the stage, which measured 300 by 200 feet and was reportedly one of the largest indoor film sets ever constructed at the time.

As the company returned home, the shooting schedule was almost two weeks behind and there was the ever-present concern over the budget. Wallis pleaded with associate producer Blanke to "go through the script again and have a talk with Keighley and see if there aren't any scenes or sequences that we can cut out of the picture." Another problem was the quality of scenes already shot in Chico. Keighley's directing style was understated and in this case underwhelming. It lacked the fast-paced, adventurous flair which was vital to convey the legendary tale. Also, many of the long shots filmed in Technicolor were out of focus. Wallis, again writing to Blanke, lambasted the director, saying: "Keighley does not know how to shoot action sequences."

Production at the Burbank studios included interior scenes of Lady Marian's quarters in Nottingham, Kent Road Tavern and the Saracen's Head Inn. By the middle of November, however, location filming began once again, this time in Pasadena at the old Busch Gardens. Smitten with the California resort town, brewer and philanthropist, Adolphus Busch purchased an ivy-draped mansion there in 1904 to escape the harsh St. Louis winters. The palatial home, aptly named *Ivy Wall*, was adjacent to undeveloped property covered in scrub brush and oak and was "a complete eyesore." Landscapers were hired to create a massive garden which was opened to the public in 1906. Other films were shot there, including *Frankenstein* and *Dr. Jekyll and Mr. Hyde* (both 1931) before the decision was made by Warner Brothers to use it as the scene of the elaborate Archery Tournament in *Robin Hood*. Keighley's once important, now defunct Jousting Scene was to have been shot there as well.

800 players were bussed to suburban Pasadena on November 22 to begin shooting. When all 800 were in their

places and the sun was exactly right, Keighley realized that there was absolutely no breeze blowing to stir the many brightly colored pennants scattered throughout the tournament field. He ordered two wind machines be hooked up, which "produced a small hurricane." The extras who were playing archers in the competition were inexperienced and didn't know where their arrows would end up when shot. Those arrows were tipped with soft rubber. The shots that counted, with arrows photographed hitting the bullseye, were steel tipped and came from the bow of Howard Hill.

Stuntman Buster Wiles met Flynn on the set of *Captain Blood* and the two became drinking buddies and friends. Like Hill, Wiles was the kind of man that Errol enjoyed spending time with, a guy's guy, rough and tumble – someone with whom Flynn could raise hell. Wiles recounted in his memoir how the trick shot of splitting an arrow during the archery tournament was devised.

> "The publicity department released the story that Howard had actually "split the arrow" in the famous tournament sequence, filmed at Busch Gardens in Pasadena. But, as great as Howard was, the publicity story was off the mark by a long shot. Howard was indeed able to strike another arrow, but the notch deflected a direct split, and it didn't photograph well. A wire was rigged in front of the Administration Building, and I fired the arrow down the wire. Now it can be revealed – Buster Wiles split the arrow!"

Wiles was just one of numerous stunt men and extras astride a horse at Busch Gardens. One columnist noted how amusing it was to hear the conversations of Prince John's mounted men-at-arms and knights. "These Norman warriors speak with Texas drawls. They're mostly ex-cowpunchers, now members of the Hollywood Riders Actors Association."

One extra caused quite a stir, just as filming in Pasadena commenced. A bit part actor named Frankie Fisher was taken into custody on the set. Fisher was listed in police records as a "known hoodlum" and an "associate of hoodlums" both in California and New York. He was seized by a newly formed gang-busting squad, developed by District Attorney Buron Fitts to fight against an influx of east coast gangsters who sought a share of the movie colony's wealth. In the raid, authorities singled Fisher out and apprehended him in the goatskin suit and leather hat of a Nottingham peasant. He was held as a material witness in the recent murder of Hymie Miller, another bit playing actor and restaurant operator. The investigator of the case, John Klein, said Fisher was a friend of Miller's, who was shot down in his bed ten days earlier.

A less serious yet costly issue on the set was significant enough to get the Screen Actors Guild involved. The organization began a policy of forbidding card-playing on movie sets due to the refusal of extras working on the *Robin Hood* shoot to stop playing while cameras were rolling. The extras, who often waited for hours, had to be called several times for scenes because they did not want to put down good hands.

Although location shooting in Pasadena didn't take as long as it had in Chico, expenses were still mounting up.

During the ten days spent at Busch Gardens, 500 box lunches were prepared per day by Katherine Higgins, manager of the Warner Brothers commissary, and her staff. Higgins compiled a list of the food consumed during the ten-day span which included: 5,000 hardboiled eggs, 4,000 apples, 1,665 loaves of bread, 5,000 cupcakes, 1,000 bananas, 500 chickens, 100 hams, 250 pounds of cheese, 10 sides of beef, one barrel of sweet pickles, 400 gallons of coffee, 5,000 half pint bottles of milk and 125 pounds of butter. The problem with the budget, however, wasn't hardboiled eggs or sweet pickles. It was Keighley.

At the end of November, the soft-spoken, sophisticated director was replaced with studio stalwart, Hungarian-born Michael Curtiz. The AP reported that Curtiz "took up the megaphone" on the *Robin Hood* set after Keighley was "stricken with influenza." Another account later that week stated the reason he left the picture when it was two-thirds completed was "an argument over a production matter on which he and his studio could not agree." The "matter" was Keighley's inability to bring the required majesty and energy to his scenes. With current budget projections swelling over $2 million and the production schedule even further behind, Wallis decided to make the change.

With most of the action sequences yet to be shot, Wallis knew that Curtiz was the one who could bring it all together with the necessary dose of dash and grandeur. Jack Warner agreed. "Unfortunately, the action sequences were not effective," Wallis explained, "and I had to replace the director in mid-production, an unheard-of event at the time.

Warner Brothers director Michael Curtiz

I felt that only Mike Curtiz could give the picture the color and scope it needed. The reason we hadn't used him in the first place was because Errol had begged us not to." According to Wallis, Flynn much preferred the "elegant and civilized" Keighley to the hard-fisted, hot-headed Curtiz.

Born in Budapest on Christmas evening, 1886, Curtiz became interested in the theater at a young age and took a job as an actor in a traveling theater company while still in his teens. He then worked as a pantomime actor in a circus before joining the National Hungarian Theater in

1912. The same year, he directed Hungary's first feature film, *Ma és holnap (Today and Tomorrow)*, in which he also had an acting role. By the 1920s Curtiz had become one of Hungary's most important and prolific directors, and in 1926, he accepted an invitation from Warner Brothers to work for them in Hollywood. While he worked steadily at the studio, first directing silent films, then talkies in the early '30s, it wasn't until 1935 and *Captain Blood* that Curtiz became one of the premiere directors at Warners. Errol Flynn would succinctly describe his relationship with the driven filmmaker:

> "I was to spend five miserable years with him, making *Robin Hood*, *Charge of the Light Brigade*, and many other films. In each he tried to make the scenes all so realistic that my skin didn't seem to matter to him. Nothing delighted him more than real bloodshed."

Curtiz, in turn, recalled his first experience with Flynn, when the actor played the part of a corpse upon his arrival in Hollywood. Said Curtiz: "Errol Flynn was an extra boy making $50 a week when I first saw him. I was making *The Case of the Curious Bride* and needed a man to walk into a darkened room to be hit on the head and lie under a piano for a whole scene. Errol was handy, so I gave him the part." A January 1935 memo from Jack Warner to Wallis begged to differ:

> "I overheard a typical Mike Curtiz-Harry Joe Brown [production supervisor] squawk about not wanting to use Errol Flynn in *The Case of the Curious Bride*. I hope that they did not change you because I want him used in this picture, first

> because I think it is a shame to let people like Curtiz and Harry Brown to even think of opposing an order from you or myself, and secondly, when we bring a man all the way from England he is at least entitled to a chance and somehow or other we haven't given him one. I want to make sure he is in the picture."

The incompatibility of Flynn and Curtiz stemmed from, among other reasons, their different approaches to movie making. Flynn was as devil-may-care off camera as his characters were on. Curtiz, on the other hand, was a consummate professional, who worked hard to perfect his craft and was an arduous taskmaster. "He was not crude or rude," observed film star Fay Wray, with whom Curtiz made two pictures, "but I felt that he was not flesh and bones, that he was part of the steel of the camera." Vincent Sherman, fellow Warner Brothers director, said of Curtiz: "His whole life was his pictures. I never heard of Mike having any personal or social relationships that mattered."

One relationship that may have mattered was with Lili Damita. Ten years before she married Flynn, she had personal and professional ties with Curtiz. In addition to making several films together in Europe, they were involved, at the very least, in a torrid affair and some sources claim were even married for a short time. Curtiz biographer, Alan K. Rode states, however, that no such evidence of a union exists. Regardless, there was no love lost between the actor and his director and there was even some wariness from Hal Wallis on assigning *Robin Hood* to Curtiz. He expressed his concerns to Blanke in one of the infamous memos.

> "There is one thing that we will have to watch with Mike. In his enthusiasm to make great shots and composition and utilize the great production values in this picture, he is, of course, more likely to go overboard than anyone else, because he just naturally loves to work with mobs and props of this kind... Also, when he gets into the fight stuff, please be sure that Mike doesn't over-shoot and get a thousand daffy shots of impossible gags, which as you know are liable to boomerang and make our scenes ridiculous."

It was not an unfounded concern, as Wallis had to complain to Curtiz about such scenes in their previous projects together, including *Captain Blood*. Among other issues, the producer was frustrated with his director over a scene between Flynn's Blood and villain Lionel Atwill. Instead of conveying Flynn's reaction of the taut scene, and the "crafty look in his eye" in an extreme closeup, Curtiz filmed the take in a long shot in order to "get the composition of a candlestick and a wine bottle on a table in the foreground," which Wallis didn't "give a damn about."

When Curtiz officially took over the film on November 30, he did so with enthusiasm and fervor. He persuaded Wallis to replace cinematographer Tony Gaudio with Sol Polito, a personal favorite, while also bringing to his team, Irving Rapper as dialogue director and Limey Plews as prop man. The details of the production to that point were relayed by the unit manager, Al Alleborn and Curtiz walked the Nottingham Castle set, lining up every shot to be filmed with Polito, who arrived early on the first day of shooting the scene. The first shot under the Curtiz regime would be a long boom, which took in the entire Castle setting.

On December 1, filming began for the Banquet Scene in Nottingham Castle. After going over everything with Curtiz and his assistant director, Jack Sullivan, Alleborn reported that the director's first day was productive and vigorous and two days later he was elated in his review of the production thus far. "I think this company with a new crew is moving along 100% better than the other crew [headed by Keighley], and everyone is endeavoring to make a comparative showing." The final version of the rambunctious banquet scene was fast-paced and exciting with Flynn at his athletic best. Wallis had warned Blanke not to let Curtiz get too outlandish with Robin's escape from Nottingham. "We must be very careful not to make the thing too wild, with Robin escaping from a hundred men," he wrote, "so the quicker he gets out of the room [in the castle] and up on the balcony the better."

The set for Gisbourne's Nottingham was designed, like everything else in the film, for Technicolor. It was a massive and impressive undertaking of medieval interior. The vast array of food for the banquet was mostly real, including the whole beef, slowly roasting on the ominous spit, "varnished at intervals to bring out its camera flavor." The huge grey stones of the castle walls were painted composition board and the heavy wooden doors were light enough for a toddler to open, so light, in fact, that an artificial squeak had to be added to make them sound heavy.

Shooting continued into the evening for several nights a week, without Flynn or de Havilland, in an attempt to make up the lost time from Keighley's tenure. In addition, some of the former director's scenes (including the initial entrance of Robin and Will Scarlet) were scheduled to be re-shot, this time with more vim and vigor. Some of the outdoor sequences were filmed at Sherwood Forest in the San Fernando Valley. The area was named accordingly, as it was the location of the 1922 Fairbanks version of *Robin Hood*. The lavish Midwick Polo and Country Club in Alhambra played host to reshoots of some of the archery tournament footage. The 208-acre club was used in part due to its facilities for housing and caring for the horses.

As filming under the Curtiz regime progressed, it was evident that Flynn wasn't the only cast member to show distaste for the director. De Havilland recalled her time under his direction with less than pleasant memories.

> "He was caustic critical, he was furious when you took an hour for lunch. You didn't take an hour for lunch with him, you took 45 minutes — 40 minutes was about all you took, because you would have to take off your costume and then you would have to go and eat something and then you would have to come back and get your makeup fixed, then you'd have to put on your costume and they were usually complicated, and you'd have to be ready for work. If instead of being 10 minutes ahead of time, you were ready on the dot, he was enraged and sulked all afternoon."

Curtiz continued to goad Flynn mercilessly as well. During a love scene, the director criticized Errol's lovemaking, remarking: "The kiss – she would not melt butter. Don't hold her like she was a hot potato. Crush her!

Maybe you break a rib! That is all right if we get a good scene." But the scenes for which Curtiz was hired are the ones in which his skills shone bright and, subsequently, Flynn's as well. The action sequences were fast-paced and thrilling and owed as much to Hill, Wiles and the others who contributed to them as they did the director and star.

Just as Howard Hill was brought in to train would-be archers, Fred Cavens was hired to impart the finer points of fencing. Belgian-born Cavens trained Flynn and Rathbone during filming of *Captain Blood* and for several weeks before *Robin Hood* began shooting, he worked with twenty-four handpicked men, rehearsing with broadswords and quarterstaffs on Warners' Stage One. His son, Albert, assisted him in the training and setting up of the sword and quarterstaff routines for the principal players. A graduate of the Belgian Military Institute, the elder Cavens was a professor of fencing at twenty-one. He began working in Hollywood as a fencing instructor, sword fight choreographer and uncredited actor during the silent film days, and was instrumental in the success of several swashbucklers starring Doug Fairbanks, Sr.

He was a meticulous trainer and was the chief influence in bringing style and technique to Hollywood screen duels. According to Cavens, movements during theatrical swordplay should be broad and magnified, unlike movements in competitive fencing, which should be as small and precise as possible. "The duel should be a fight and not a fencing exhibition," he explained, "and should disregard at times classically correct guards and lunges." He believed that on film, the natural fighting instinct should come through as the dominant factor. "When this occurs," he said, "the whole performance will leave an impression of strength, skill and natural grace." On the *Robin Hood* set, liberties were taken with technique in relation to historic time period. The medieval broad blades used in the movie were very heavy and hacking weapons and the elegant fencing techniques incorporated by Cavens weren't developed until centuries later.

Curtiz loved the use of scenery and props to heighten the drama and violence of his duels and Robin Hood gave him ample opportunity to engage this technique. Flynn and Rathbone cross their swords down a winding castle staircase, as well as knocking over a giant candelabra and slashing their blades through dripping candles. The director engaged Polito's camera skills to capture the large, violent shadows of the fighting men on a stone column. With Cavens' guidance, Flynn looked good with a sword and had shed the awkwardness shown in *Captain Blood*. He did not have the patience or discipline for regular practice, but he was a quick study and, at twenty-eight, had a natural athletic prowess which bode him well. Rathbone, on the other hand, had developed a sincere interest in fencing since appearing in *Captain Blood* and studied with Cavens for several years to become a fine swordsman. "He has excellent form and is the most colorful of all the people I have taught," exclaimed Cavens. "I doubt that he would do well in competition, but for picture purposes he is better than the best fencer in the world."

In his memoirs, Flynn boasted that he performed all his own stunts in the film, but he had help from both Buster

Star pupil Basil Rathbone working with fencing instructor, Fred Cavens

Wiles and his Warner Brothers double, Don Turner, who was used in some of the sword fight scenes with Sir Guy. Although Rathbone did his own fencing, he used a stunt double, Fred Graham, for one of the film's most crucial scenes. Graham had worked as Clark Gable's stand-in on *Mutiny on the Bounty* at MGM before moving over to Warner Brothers, where his first assignment was as double for Rathbone in *Robin Hood*. For his initial studio project, he would break his ankle taking Rathbone's fall from the castle staircase in the final duel between Sir Guy and Robin.

After taking the directorial reins, Curtiz studied every movement in front of the camera and kept a sharp eye as Errol was given still more fencing lessons and continually coached by archer Howard Hill. When Hill scored a bull's eye, Flynn sidled up to Curtiz, slapped him on the back and said: "Good, wasn't I, sport? The irritated Hungarian muttered "sohn of a beetch" and tried to ignore the interruption. Flynn was better behaved as filming progressed, however, wanting to wrap it up in order to get out to sea on his yacht, the *Sirocco*. He was also pleased with his increased financial standing. His first comedy, *The Perfect Specimen*, was released in October and proved a relative success. As a result, Warners' drew up a new seven years option contract for its rapidly rising star that increased his weekly rate to $2,250 from his previous rate of $800.

After more than four months of filming, the production finally closed on January 14, 1938. It was a long day, over eighteen continuous hours. Al Aleborn reported, "Curtiz company called 8:30 A.M. ...finished shooting at 3:10 A.M. this morning." After an additional day of filming to tie up some loose ends, the final tally was 38 days over schedule and significantly over budget. It was the most expensive picture ever to be made at Warner Brothers up to that time. It had better be worth it.

SET IT TO MUSIC AND
SEND IT TO THE MASSES

Composer Erich Wolfgang Korngold and Basil Rathbone during the NBC radio broadcast of Korngold's *Robin Hood* score

Jack Warner knew it was worth it. Less than a week after filming wrapped and before editing or scoring the picture had begun, Warner rewarded Curtiz with a $2,500 bonus. He instructed the studio attorney, Roy Obringer, to raise the director's pay. "When we exercise the next option of Mike Curtiz's contract," Warner wrote, "he goes to $2,600 per week commencing May 1938. We are now giving him a $200 weekly bonus. On this date, May 26, I want you to increase this bonus to $400, making it a flat sum of $3,000 weekly." Just as with Flynn, the financial increase was a testament to the economic impact made by Curtiz, under the watch of frugal Warner. For his contribution to *Robin Hood,* the director also got a bump in his relationship with Hal Wallis, who became a "more fervent advocate of Curtiz" and never forgot how he came through for him on *Robin Hood*. In his autobiography, Wallis went as far as claiming that Curtiz was his "favorite director then and always."

The director had done much to warrant such studio accolades, not the least of which was to get the picture completed and with plenty of vigor and excitement in the final product to boot. Olivia de Havilland, who held no personal affection for Curtiz, would reflect on the success of the film and reluctantly give the director his due. "Oh, Curtiz was a Hungarian Otto Preminger and that's that," she declared. "He was a tyrant, he was abusive, he was cruel. Oh, he was a villain, but I guess he was pretty good. We didn't believe it then, but he clearly was. He knew what he was doing. He knew how to tell a story very clearly and he knew how to keep things going; you had to transmit vitality. I was astounded by *Robin Hood*'s vitality, it's effervescence. That was a revelation, and I thought, well, he had something to do with it, and he did. I have to admit that."

When filming was complete, the arduous task of editing began. A rough cut had been assembled during production, but Wallis wanted to edit the work himself to get an even faster pace to the action. His numerous notes on what scenes to cut were filled with comments like: "Trim just a little – a few frames, a half a foot, a foot, or whatever is necessary on all the cuts from the shooting of the first arrow in the gallows sequence." With the editing and Technicolor transfer underway, it was time to have the film scored to music.

Wallis admitted his musical tastes "ran to classical themes and strong orchestral scores." He knew that he wanted Erich Wolfgang Korngold to produce the musical background for *Robin Hood*. He first met Korngold in 1934 at the castle of Max Reinhardt near Salzburg in 1934, when the producers were in the process of bringing Reinhardt's version of *A Midsummer Night's Dream* to the screen. "He [Korngold] played the piano for us there one evening," Wallis recalled, "Unforgettable music of concert quality... I was impressed with his genius." Wallis later declared the composer's scores to be virtual symphonies and Reinhardt invited him to the United States to adapt the music of Felix Mendelssohn for *A Midsummer Night's Dream*.

As a result of his successful work for Reinhardt and Warner Brothers, Korngold was invited back to Hollywood (the Jewish-born composer lived in Austria) by Paramount to work on its operatic musical, *Give Us This Night*. At this point, the composer's work had been banned in Germany by the Nazis, which cut off his income from music royalties. With his finances in dire straits he couldn't refuse Paramount's offer and he and his family moved to California. While working on *Give Us This Night*, Wallis asked Korngold if he would be interested in writing an original score for the swashbuckling epic, *Captain Blood*. He eventually accepted the offer and his work on *Blood* garnered him an Oscar nomination. He would win the award the following year for the score of his next picture, Warners' *Anthony Adverse*. After working yet again for the studio in *The Prince and the Pauper*, Korngold returned to Austria in 1937 to compose his new opera, *Die Kathrin*. He was arranging the opera's premiere in January 1938 when he received a cable from Hal Wallis to come back to Hollywood within ten days to score *The Adventures of Robin Hood*. With the premiere of his opera postponed until autumn, Korngold accepted the offer and made his way out of Austria.

Tensions were high in Europe with Hitler's presence looming. The Korngolds headed for the port of Le Havre to set sail for the United States, but the journey was treacherous, with the winter weather offering icy roads and bitter cold, while at every border the couple was stopped and questioned. They finally made it to New York in early February, only to have the train they were taking to the west coast collide with an automobile just outside of Pasadena. The couple arrived in Los Angeles and rented a house in the Toluca Lake district, which was a ten-minute walk from Warner Brothers, allowing Korngold the opportunity to walk to work if he chose. The next day the composer viewed a rough cut of the film at the studio and became painfully aware that he could not be involved in such a fast-paced adventure picture.

Three days after the screening, Korngold hand delivered to Wallis a carefully crafted letter of rejection, regretfully turning down the assignment.

> "I am sincerely sorry to have to bother you once more. I do appreciate deeply your kindness and

courtesy toward me, and I am aware of the fact that you have made all concessions possible to facilitate my work.

But please believe a desperate man who has to be true to himself and to you, a man who knows what he can do and what he cannot do. *Robin Hood* is no picture for me. I have no relation to it and therefore cannot produce any music for it. I am a musician of the heart, of passions and psychology; I am not a musical illustrator of a 90% action picture.... Therefore, let me say "no" definitely, and let me say it today when no time has been lost for you as yet, since the work print will not be ready until tomorrow. And please do not try to make me change my mind; my resolve is unshakable.... I implore you not to be angry with me and not to deprive me of your friendship."

The next day word came from Europe that the Austrian chancellor, Kurt Schuschnigg was meeting with Hitler, setting into motion the *Anschluss*, the annexation of Austria into Nazi Germany. The same day, Leo Forbstein, head of Warner Brothers' music department, arrived at Korngold's home and, at the behest of Jack Warner, Wallis and Henry Blanke, pleaded with the composer to take the job. "You have to do it," he urged. Taking into consideration the stunning news he had just received regarding his homeland, Korngold accepted the offer, but not before negotiating terms which would allow him to work on a weekly basis, with the understanding that he could leave the film at the end of any given week. Two days later, Blanke sent out a memo to all concerned that Korngold was "definitely set to do the music on *Robin Hood*." Within weeks his property in Austria was confiscated by the Nazis ("for his numerous debts" was the official reason), and Korngold and his family remained in the United States through the end of World War II. The composer credited *The Adventures of Robin Hood* with saving his life and would later reflect on this period, saying: "We thought of ourselves as Viennese; Hitler made us Jewish."

Realizing early in filming that more time might be needed to complete the project, Jack Warner arranged an extension in October 1937 from MGM for the release date. The originally agreed on date of February 14 was extended to "before June 1," and Warner finally settled on May 14 for the picture's general release. This allowed Korngold seven weeks to compose and record the score for a project he still felt his talents weren't suited. His son George recalled years later how the stress affected Korngold during the period: "My father was on the verge of stopping several times," he said. "I shall never forget his anguished protestations of 'I just can't do it!' which I overheard in the middle of the night through my bedroom wall. He was suffering, and at the same time producing one of his finest scores."

Korngold, by his own admission, found his true niche in opera and his approach to film scores was operatic. Film historian Tony Thomas described his score to *Robin Hood* as "practically an opera minus a libretto." Almost two-thirds of the movie's running time is supported by music and Thomas hailed Korngold's score as "a textbook example of what music can do for a film." The flow and

A promotional archery tournament between Radio City Rockettes and Corps de Ballet atop the Radio Music Hall, May 1938

buoyancy of the score help enhance the story and characters.

The final music for *The Adventures of Robin Hood* was exquisite. The lushness of Korngold's creation evoked the splendor and romance of Sherwood Forest and all areas adjacent. He made an artform of the film score by weaving the music throughout the picture to enhance the rich visuals with equally descriptive notes and creating musical character themes. The studio realized what a splendid work Korngold had produced and saw the potential to use it as a marketing tool.

In 1925, two years after founding Warner Brothers Pictures Incorporated, the studio launched its own radio station, KFWB, in Los Angeles, to publicize and promote its film product. Warner stars were expected to appear over the air at KFWB to discuss and advertise their latest movies. To utilize Korngold's majestic music and their own recording equipment, a special broadcast was planned for early May 1938, to build anticipation for the upcoming premiere of *Robin Hood*. The presentation would include ten sequences chosen by the composer from the film's score. On the afternoon of May 11, under Korngold's guidance, the 50-piece Warner Brothers' Orchestra recorded the chosen music and a live performance was broadcast coast to coast that evening over radio station KECA and the NBC Blue Network. The distinctive voice of Basil Rathbone was used to narrate the piece. Plans to distribute the broadcast commercially were abandoned, though a handful of pressings were produced for Korngold and several Warner Brothers executives.

With a record amount of money invested in the film, the *Robin Hood* radio broadcast wasn't the first publicity-related event to showcase the upcoming picture. The studio staged a Robin Hood Ball on Saturday, April 23. The event was held at Charles Farrell's Racquet Club in Palm Springs as a preliminary to the Robin Hood Archery Tournament to be held the following day at the Desert Inn resort. To bolster the publicity for the tournament, Warners transported representatives from several movie magazines and scores of newspapers to Palm Springs. When they arrived, the press corps took part in their own bow-and-arrow contest, in which, as one columnist observed, "Some of 'em hit the target; most of 'em didn't, but they all penned stories."

The official match was a rousing success of attention-grabbing, with some 300 spectators seated along the turf of the golf course under brightly colored umbrellas. The contest, sponsored by the National Archery Association, was open to female archers from California schools and colleges and archery clubs all over the country, many gaily clad in Robin Hood-like attire. Warner Brothers peppered the grounds with many of its stars and contract players, a common practice of studios to promote its films. The Warner luminaries including Dick Powell, Joan Blondell, Rosemary Lane and young starlets Susan Hayward and Carole Landis (who would leave Warners shortly thereafter for Paramount and 20th Century-Fox, respectively). Also on hand was Patric Knowles, one of the few representatives of the film's cast, and Basil Rathbone, who presented the winning trophies. Ironically among the celebrity set in attendance was James Cagney, original choice for Robin, who strangely appeared with Rathbone and some of the lady archers in promotional photos. Howard Hill acted as one of the tournament's judges, as well as performing several difficult exhibition shots, including shooting pencils and even matches from a distance of twenty feet.

As Robin Hood and archery were synonymous, yet another contest was held to advertise the upcoming debut of the film. On the roof of Radio City Music Hall, where the world premiere of the film was to be hosted on May 12, thirty-five Radio City Rockettes lined up in front of one archery target and thirty-five ballerinas from the Corps de Ballet lined up in front of another to compete with bow and arrow. The fun promotion ended with the young ladies chasing their green hats labeled *The Adventures of Robin*

Hood around the rooftop due to several gusts of wind. Stunts like these events were just the tip of the film exploitation iceberg, as the studio had appropriated $100,000 for advertising the picture, the largest amount in the company's history. The mammoth marketing campaign included ad space in newspapers, magazines and trade publications and billboard postings were scheduled in over 4,000 cities across the country.

Preparations for the pictures general release on May 14 were just as elaborate. An exhibit of the original sketches of the castle sets used in the film was installed in the foyer of the Radio City Music Hall, and a record number of Technicolor prints was ordered by the studio for the openings in 300 US cities. Plans were made for a simultaneous premiere in Los Angeles which were announced to include Flynn and de Havilland. The two stars of the film not only didn't attend the premieres, neither was even in the country when the movie was released.

Production on *Robin Hood* was long and laborious and both Errol and Olivia were exhausted and ready for filming to end. Less than a month after completing the picture, however, the onscreen couple was reteamed in a modern-day screwball comedy, the complete opposite spectrum from *Robin Hood*. The film, *Four's a Crowd*, also reunited the duo with their *RH* co-star, Patric Knowles, as well as with Curtiz, who was slated to direct. Frustrated with back-to-back productions, annoyed at playing merely the love interest in yet another Flynn vehicle and being directed again by Curtiz, de Havilland's nerves were thin. She began

**Classic swordplay between Flynn and Rathbone.
Both actors were trained by fencing expert, Fred Cavens**

showing up late to the set and forgetting her lines. The pressure came to a head in late February when she "walked off the set and refused to work any longer," after being there until 6:45 pm. Her exhaustion called for a medical exam and a cardiogram showed the actress suffered from severe arrythmia and fibrillation. She was also anemic, had low blood pressure and was underweight. The studio's doctor, W.R. Meals, informed Hal Wallis that if Olivia continued working at her grueling pace she could be "rendered permanently ill." When the studio disregarded his instruction, de Havilland responded with continued lateness to the set and refusal to work at night. The situation got so bad that studio manager Tenney Wright sent a memo directly to Jack Warner. "I suggest this matter be turned over to the Actors Guild," he wrote, "to have them police Miss de Havilland." When production ended, the actress was in desperate need of rest, and she and her mother left immediately for England on the French ocean liner, the *Normandie*.

Like his costar, Flynn wasted no time after the completion of *Four's a Crowd*. He flew to Miami to join Lili for his long awaited "cruise to nowhere" on the *Sirocco*, which would actually consist of six weeks in the Caribbean. The trip had to be postponed three days, however, when the vessel went into drydock after two lifeboats were lost in a gale which left four feet of water in the hold. The setback merely extended the trip and delayed his hesitant return to Hollywood, hence missing any of the *Robin Hood* release hoopla.

De Havilland and her mother arrived back in New York on the *Normandie* on May 16, better rested and ready for several public appearances arranged by the studio to promote *Robin Hood*. Two days after her arrival, she attended a cocktail party held in her honor and hosted by the managing director of Radio City Music Hall. After the reception, she, Mrs. de Havilland and Herb Crooker, Warner publicity director, left for Philadelphia, where she would play guest of honor at a luncheon with the local press. The whirlwind tour led to Pittsburg then wrapped up in Cleveland before the actress made her way back to California.

An April sneak preview of the film in Pomona, near Los Angeles, proved to be a sensation. Jack Warner telegrammed studio executives in New York bursting with pride. "In history of our company," Warner gushed, "never have we had picture that scored in front of audience like this did." On its opening day at the Music Hall, the film made box-office history, beating the record of Walt Disney's *Snow White and the Seven Dwarfs*, set earlier that year. By four o'clock in the afternoon the attendance exceeded that for the *Snow White* opening and early in the evening the Music Hall management estimated the expected take to be about $14,000 for the day. *Snow White* grossed $12,000 the first day. On the west coast, Warner Brothers' Hollywood and Downtown theaters saw their best business in seven years, and the picture established a house record at several theaters across the country including the Fox in San Francisco.

Warners wasted no time announcing a sequel, tentatively titled *Sir Robin of Locksley*. Preparations for a Technicolor spectacle starring Flynn and directed by Curtiz were hailed before the original had even hit screens. In the autumn, young Irish actress, Geraldine Fitzgerald, recently signed by Warner Brothers, was publicized for the female lead. The film, however, would never come to fruition, though several non-Flynn sequels or retellings of the legend would be produced.

With the movie being held over for several weeks at theaters across the country, its popularity with audiences was obvious and critics joined the masses in their collective glowing reviews. *Variety* raved, "It is cinematic pageantry at its best, a highly imaginative telling of folklore in all the hues of Technicolor." *Harrison's Reports* followed suit, saying: "Excellent entertainment! Not only does it show great care in production, that is, in lavish settings, fine technicolor photography, expert direction and acting but also in the manner in which the story has been developed." Frank S. Nugent of the *New York Times* said the film is "a richly produced, bravely bedecked, romantic and colorful show, it leaps boldly to the forefront of this year's best." Nugent even acknowledged the entertainment value provided by the film's villains, writing: "...how the children's matinees will hiss them! We couldn't. We enjoyed them all too much."

In February 1939, 1250 people gathered at the Biltmore Bowl, the grand ballroom in Los Angeles' Biltmore Hotel for the 11th Academy Awards ceremony. *The Adventures of Robin Hood* was nominated for four of the coveted prizes: Best Picture, Best Art Direction (Carl Jules Weyl), Best Film Editing (Ralph Dawson) and Best Original Score for Korngold. All won except for the most-envied Best Picture, which would have been represented by Hal Wallis and Henry Blanke. Wallis did gain recognition, however, copping the prestigious Irving G. Thalberg Memorial Award, established the previous year for "consistently high quality of motion picture production." The final cost to produce the film was just over $2,000,000 and it grossed almost twice that amount during its initial 1938 release, Warner Brothers' biggest financial hit of the year.

Including *The Adventures of Robin Hood*, Errol Flynn and Olivia de Havilland made a total of eight films together. Their movies are some of the best-remembered from both Warner Brothers and Hollywood's golden era. According to de Havilland, she never saw *Robin Hood* upon its initial release. Like many of her movie star peers, she cranked out picture after picture, never watching the final product. When she did finally see it, in Paris in 1959, she was struck at how good it was, and she wrote a letter to Flynn telling him how impressed she was and how dismissive she had been of it. "An apology twenty years late," she later recalled. "But I tore it up. I reconsidered, deciding Errol would think I was silly. I'll always be sorry. A few months later he was dead. Seeing *Robin Hood* after all these years made me realize how good all our adventure films were, and I wrote Errol that I was glad I had been in every scene of them. I was astounded at *Robin Hood*'s vitality, its effervescence. I thought it was simply wonderful. It was a revelation to me. It was classic."

Other Books on Classic Movies by Rupert Alistair

Girl Next Door: The Life and Career of Jeanne Crain

Sin and Vice in Black & White: 15 Classic Pre-Code Movies

The Name Below the Title: 20 Classic Movie Character Actors from Hollywood's Golden Age

The Name Below the Title, Volume 2: 20 MORE Classic Movie Character Actors from Hollywood's Golden Age

Hollywood and the Home Front: 25 Fabulous Films from the Forties

The Search for Scarlett O'Hara: Gone with the Wind and Hollywood's Most Famous Casting Call

Classic Movies: 14 Films You May Not Have Seen, But Should

Classic Movie Gems: 16 MORE Films You May Not Have Seen, But Should

Hidden Hollywood Gold

Notes & References

Let's Make Cagney, Robin Hood!

1. "Don't you think": Behlmer, *Inside Warner Brothers (1935 – 1951)*, page 44
2. Top Ten Moneymakers in Hollywood: Warren, Cagney. *Cagney: The Authorized Biography*, page 114
3. Donat would arrive in Hollywood: "Donat Set for 'Robin Hood'." *The Film Daily*, February 14, 1935, page 14
4. The Donat project: *Motion Picture Daily*, July 15, 1935, page 18
5. MGM began developing a musical: Behlmer, "From Legend to Film," *Introduction to The Adventures of Robin Hood*, page 12
6. with a purchase amount of $30,000: "'Robin Hood' for MGM," *Motion Picture Daily*, August 14, 1935, page 11
7. Wallis also assigned Dr. Herman Lissauer: Behlmer, "From Legend to Film," *Introduction to The Adventures of Robin Hood*, page 13
8. Louella Parsons announced: *Reading Times*, August 19, 1935, page 7
9. running a full-page ad: *Motion Picture Daily*, August 26, 1935
10. production was scheduled: *Motion Picture Daily*, August 26, 1935, page 18
11. Curtiz became easily exasperated: Higham, *The Warner Brothers*, page 121
12. His contract stipulated: Ibid, page 88
13. English star Leslie Howard: Behlmer, *Inside Warner Brothers*, page 21

14. He had already become fascinated: Higham, *The Warner Brothers*, page 121
15. Flynn was "amateurish: Ibid
16. *Variety* announced that Flynn: "Warners Stands Off Cagney, Spots Flynn." *Variety*, February 5, 1936, page 3
17. "let Cagney know": Behlmer, *Inside Warner Brothers*, page 44
18. The rogue star's salary: "Warners Stands Off Cagney, Spots Flynn." *Variety*, February 5, 1936, page 3
19. Cagney – with court approval: "Cagney Suit Against Warner Up Feb 25." *Independent Exhibiters Film Bulletin*, February 19, 1936, page 7
20. The agreement allowed Warner: Behlmer, *Introduction to The Adventures of Robin Hood*, page 17-18
21. They suggested caution: "'Robin Hood' Filmers Check Data to Make Old Story Authentic." *East Liverpool Evening Review*, December 1, 1937, page 6
22. "The development of the romance: Behlmer, *Introduction to The Adventures of Robin Hood*, page 18
23. Maid Marian be omitted completely: Behlmer, *America's Favorite Movies: Behind the Scenes*, page 64
24. "You cannot have the maid: Behlmer, *Introduction to The Adventures of Robin Hood*, page 18
25. He was given the story material: Behlmer, *Introduction to The Adventures of Robin Hood*, page 20
26. His own approach was very evident: Ibid
27. This draft portrayed Sir Robin of Locksley: Winters, *Erich Wolfgang Korngold's The Adventures of Robin Hood: A Film Score Guide*, page 56

28. Refined and urbane, Keighley: Rode, *Michael Curtiz: A Life in Film*, page 211
29. Wallis informed Blanke: Behlmer, *America's Favorite Movies: Behind the Scenes*, page 70
30. "Listen, a picture": "Warner Brothers," *Fortune* magazine, December 1937, page 110, 115

Errol and Olivia

31. "a magnificent specimen": Niven, *Bring on the Empty Horses*, page 124
32. "He had mediocre talent": Warner, *My First Hundred Years in Hollywood*, page 232
33. He was described by his mother: Flynn, *My Wicked, Wicked Ways*, page 25
34. Flynn would later confess: Ibid, page 30
35. His mother's people: Ibid, page 33
36. "I was bigger than most: Ibid, page 41
37. Within a year: McNulty, *The Life and Career of Errol Flynn*, page 12-13
38. Errol was given a temporary position: Moore, *The Young Errol: Flynn Before Hollywood*, page 30
39. I could commit lines: Flynn, *My Wicked, Wicked Ways*, page 107
40. Signed today: Thomas, Behlmer, McCarty. *The Films of Errol Flynn*, page 23
41. "Everything about her: Flynn, *My Wicked, Wicked Ways*, page 187
42. "Girls and hero-worshipping": Whitington, "Errol Flynn – Adventurer." *Sydney Morning Herald*, March 31, 1936, page 5
43. "We were poles apart": Flynn, *My Wicked, Wicked Ways*, page 198
44. Their parents' marriage: Fontaine, *No Bed of Roses*, page 7

45. Due to her daughters' poor health: Thomas, *The Films of Olivia de Havilland*, page 22
46. "I saw a girl": Warner, Jennings, *My First Hundred Years on Hollywood*, page 234
47. Jean Muir was the original pick: Thomas, Behlmer, *The Films of Errol Flynn*, page 67
48. Anita Louise was mentioned: *The Film Daily*, March 23, 1936, page 8
49. *Variety* reported that de Havilland: *Variety*, June 3, 1936, page 7
50. "we must insist on using de Havilland:" Behlmer, *Inside Warner Brothers*, page 31
51. Louise was eventually paired: *Fresno Bee*, July 2, 1936, page 14
52. Warner hated for any contract player: Rode, *Michael Curtiz: A Life in Film*, page 213
53. Wallis gave strict instructions: Behlmer, *Inside Warner Brothers*, page 46
54. "Miss Louise recently: "Star and Starlet in Reported Feud." *Harrisburg Telegraph*, December 1, 1937, page 8
55. "Together these two amateurs": Warner, Jennings. *My First Hundred Years on Hollywood*, page 235
56. When Jean Muir tested: Higham, *Sisters: The Story of Olivia de Havilland and Joan Fontaine*, page 53
57. "By the time we made": Flynn, *My Wicked, Wicked Ways*, page 208
58. under his newly signed: (Sheila Graham's column, *The Herald* (Melbourne), November 18, 1937, page 36
59. "soothing voice": Curtis, *James Whale: A New World of Gods and Monsters*, page 202
60. "all the henna": Skal, *Claude Rains: An Actor's Voice*, 2009
61. When McDowell confessed: Ibid

62. $2,000 a week: Paul Harrison's *In Hollywood* column, *Wilkes-Barre Times Leader*, July 31, 1937, page 16
63. $6,000 by April 1938: *Picture Play*, "Star Salaries." April 1938, page 77
64. "He was monstrously lazy": Rathbone, *In and Out of Character*, page 151
65. "Flynn's boon companion in debauchery": Aberth, *A Knight at the Movies: Medieval History on Film*, page 170

Welcome to Sherwood!

66. "I wonder if we are wrong": Behlmer, *Inside Warner Brothers*, 1985, page 46
67. Also, in tow were fifty horses: Wallace, "He Robbed the Rich and Gave to the Poor," *Silver Screen* Magazine, January 1938, page 28
68. fleet of forty trucks: "Record Budget Approved for 'Robin Hood' in Color." *Brooklyn Daily Eagle*, September 14, 1937, page 6
69. More than 20,000 items: "100,000 Props for Robin Hood." *International Photographer*, October 1937, page 31
70. The studio was able to save: Ibid
71. Tons of foodstuffs: *Motion Picture Herald*, October 9, 1937, page 29
72. Key technical staff arrived: "100 Actors to Be Here for Robin Hood Picture." *Chico Enterprise*, Sept. 15, 1937
73. steel reinforced artificial trees: Wallace, "He Robbed the Rich and Gave to the Poor," *Silver Screen* Magazine, January 1938, page 28

74. Stables were built: Higham, *Errol Flynn: The Untold Story*, page 104
75. "Kindly have a talk": Behlmer, *America's Favorite Movies: Behind the Scenes*, page 72
76. Employees at the Richardson Springs: Moon, *Chico: Life and Times of a City of Fortune*, page 138
77. the crew would watch movies: Brannen, Emily. Newsreview.com: Local Stories. November 9, 2006
78. When an eleven-year-old: Obituary of Dorothy Mae Rigel, June 28, 2015
79. "He was such a good actor": Flynn, *My Wicked, Wicked Ways*, page 299
80. "passion for unnecessary detail": Higham, *Errol Flynn: The Untold Story*, page 104
81. "At the rate of three days": Behlmer, *Inside Warner Brothers*, page 49
82. when noisy rapids: "Creek Silencer to Check Noise of Rapids." *Sunday Times Signal* (Zanesville, Ohio), October 31, 1937, page 13
83. Pallette's 280 pounds: "Film Actor Hurt." *Miami Daily News-Record*, September 30, 1937, page 1
84. "One Sunday there were thousands": "He Robbed the Rich and Gave to the Poor." *Silver Screen*, January 1938, page 29
85. As the citizenry: *Santa Cruz Sentinel*, November 3, 1937, page 3
86. 103 local men: McNulty, *The Life and Career of Errol Flynn*, page 58
87. Raine felt Keighley's ideas: Behlmer, *Inside Warner Brothers*, page 47
88. "Christ's second coming": Ibid, page 48
89. "Ungentlemanly Technicolor": "Color Over Hollywood," *The Screen Guilds' Magazine*, July 1935, page 7

90. *Variety* held little hope: *Variety*, Film Reviews, January 13, 1937, page 13
91. *Film Bulletin* claimed: *Independent Exhibitors Film Bulletin* 1938, page 6
92. For the art department: "'Robin Hood' Filmers Check Data to Make Old Story Authentic." *East Liverpool Evening Review*, December 1, 1937, page 6
93. He realized his interest: Jorgensen, Scoggins. *Creating the Illusion: A Fashionable History of Hollywood Costume Designers*, page 73
94. "Milo knew what worked": Mann, *Behind the Screen: How Gays and Lesbians Shaped Hollywood, 1910-1969*, page 243
95. After chain mesh armor: Craig, Carol. "A New Robin Hood," *Motion Picture*. January 1938, page 60
96. The final tally: "Designers of Women's Wear Emphasize Jewelry Elegance." *The Pantagraph*, February 6, 1938, page 14
97. an estimated $10,000: *Winnipeg Tribune*, December 18, 1938, page 19

Robin at Play

98. A forty-yard archery range: *Collier's* magazine, Vol. 102, 1938, p. 63
99. He was, however, reported: "Howard Hill, County's Famous Marksman." *Shelby County Reporter* (Columbiana, Alabama), May 20, 1937, page 2
100. The skilled marksman: *Forest and Outdoors, Canadian Forestry Association*, 1938, "Robin Hood Shoots Again" by Kerry Wood, pp 329
101. Also, a wonderful trick shot: Ibid, page 330
102. Hill played semi-pro baseball: Atwill, Lionel. "The World's Greatest Archer," *Field & Stream*, June 1998, page 158

103. After its release, he rigorously promoted: Smith, Jerry C. "Howard Hill: World's Greatest Archer." October 1, 2014 http://discoverstclair.com/st-clair-history/howard-hill/
104. He was paid $100 a week: Atwill, Lionel. "The World's Greatest Archer," *Field & Stream*, June 1998, page 160
105. Hill spent numerous hours: Recounted by Jerry Hill, nephew of Howard Hill – Traditional Archery Society Website: https://www.traditionalarcherysociety.com/post/errol-flynn-howard-hill-7290723
106. He, Hill and a Chico resident: "Movie Star Shoots Wrong Kind of Bird." *San Bernardino Sun*, October 15, 1937, page 17
107. the studio's publicity office: "Star Shoots Wildcat with Bow and Arrow." *San Bernardino Sun*, October 21, 1937, page 3
108. While hunting, Errol's dog flushed: "Movie Star Kills Cat with Arrow." *Chico Enterprise*, October 18, 1937
109. Later reports acknowledged: "Modern Heroes Shown by Hollywood Formula." *Fresno Bee The Republican*, December 12, 1937, page 28
110. "Errol Flynn was my friend": Knowles, "Rebuttal for a Friend" Epilogue from *The Spy Who Never Was*, Thomas, page 171-2
111. The owner, Bill Miller: Ibid, page 172
112. The duo began to receive: Ibid, page 173
113. "The stranger was": Ibid, page 174
114. She arrived in early October: McNulty, *The Life and Career of Errol Flynn*, page 60-61
115. "Lili Damita is taking no chances": Sheila Graham's Column, *Washington, DC Evening Star*, October 8, 1937, page C-7

116. Upon her arrival: Rode, *Michael Curtiz: A Life in Film*, page 214
117. "Lili was so violently: Flynn, *My Wicked, Wicked Ways*, page 209
118. "If Errol Flynn and Lili Damita: *Picture Play*, May 1937, "Hollywood High Lights," page 41
119. She arrived in Chico: Amburn, *Olivia de Havilland and the Golden Age of Hollywood*, page 50
120. It was the first time: *Ogden Standard-Examiner*, November 28, 1937, page 23
121. Initially hired by Warner Brothers: "The Story of Ann Robinson – Stand-In." *Silver Screen* Magazine, April 1938, page 79
122. The two women were friends: Higham, *Sisters*, page 81
123. "Yes, we did fall in love": "Errol Flynn? He never had his wicked way with me, says Gone with The Wind star Olivia de Havilland." Daily Mail.com, June 17, 2009, https://www.dailymail.co.uk/tvshowbiz/article-1193489/Errol-Flynn-He-wicked-way-says-Gone-With-The-Wind-star-Olivia-Havilland.html)
124. "I didn't reject him": "Golden Girl: The Divine Olivia de Havilland." The Independent, July 14, 2009, https://www.independent.co.uk/arts-entertainment/films/features/golden-girl-the-divine-olivia-de-havilland-1744807.html
125. "I thought, well I'm going to torture Errol Flynn": Olivia de Havilland Interview – *The Adventures of Errol Flynn* DVD, Movies Unlimited
126. Every morning at 5 a.m.: Higham, *Sisters*, page 71
127. A week after her arrival: "Olivia de Havilland Influenza Victim." *Oakland Tribune*, October 30, 1937, page 3

128. Early in production: *Wilkes-Barre Evening News*, September 8, 1937, page 8
129. "I loathe the bloody thing": Behlmer, *Inside Warner Brothers*, page 49
130. "I feel like one of the oldest": Ibid
131. "She seems to have gone elegant": Telegram from Wallis to Keighley, November 1, 1937, USC Warner Brothers Archive

Trouble at the Helm

132. Posters went up around town: Lorenzen, Annis. "Magic Town: Museum exhibit celebrates the movies made in Chico." June 14, 2001, Newsreview.com
133. Carrying the dateline: *Ogden Standard-Examiner*, November 17, 1937, page 9
134. The reimagined Nottingham Castle: "Rebuild Famous Castle for New Film, Robin Hood." *Harrisburg Telegraph*, December 1, 1937, page 9
135. "go through the script again": Behlmer, *Inside Warner Brothers*, page 50
136. "Keighley does not know": Interoffice Memo from Wallis to Blanke, November 3, 1937, USC Warner Brothers Archive
137. Smitten with the California: Vincent, Roger. "Busch's Long-Brewing Presence," *Los Angeles Times*, June 13, 2008
138. 800 players were bussed: "Pasadena Becomes Village of Nottingham." *The Evening Herald* (Klamath Falls, Oregon), November 22, 1937, page 7
139. "The publicity department released": Wiles, Donati, *My Days with Errol Flynn*, page 77
140. "These Norman warriors speak": Paul Harrison's column, *Rhinelander Daily News*, December 2, 1937, page 18

141. A bit part actor named Frankie Fisher: "Robin Hood Loses Tilt with the Law." *Oakland Tribune*. November 23, 1937, page 21; "Actor Seized in L.A. Roundup." *San Bernardino County Sun*. November 23, 1937, page 2
142. The organization began a policy: *Sydney Morning Herald*, February 8, 1938, page 29
143. During the ten days: "The Extras Lunch with Extra Zest." *The Emporia Gazette*, December 25, 1937, page 4
144. The AP reported that Curtiz: *San Pedro News Pilot*, December 1, 1937, page 8
145. "an argument over a production matter": *Fresno Bee*, December 5, 1937, page 22
146. Jack Warner agreed: Rode, page 215
147. "Unfortunately, the action sequences": Wallis, Higham, *Starmaker: The Autobiography of Hal B. Wallis*, page 54
148. "I was to spend five miserable years": Flynn, *Wicked Ways*, page 202
149. "Errol Flynn was an extra boy": Meyer, *Warner Brothers Directors: The Hard-Boiled, the Comic and the Weepers*, page 82
150. "I overheard a typical": Behlmer, *Inside Warner Brothers*, page 19
151. "He was not crude": Harmetz, *Round Up the Usual Suspects*, page 126
152. "His whole life was his pictures": Ibid, page 75
153. Curtiz biographer, Alan K. Rode: Rode, page 68
154. "There is one thing": Behlmer, *Inside Warner Bros.*, page 53
155. Instead of conveying Flynn's reaction: Ibid, page 23
156. The details of the production: Ibid, page 53
157. "I think this company": Ibid, page 52

158. "We must be very careful": Ibid, page 51
159. The vast array of food: *Rutland Daily Herald*, December 14, 1937, page 10
160. The lavish Midwick Polo and Country Club: Rode, page 216-17
161. "He was caustic critical": Reed, Rochelle, ed. Olivia de Havilland. *Dialogue on Film*, Beverly Hills, California; Center for Advanced Film Studies, American Film Institute, 1974, page 56
162. "The kiss – she would not melt butter": Meyer, page 87
163. His son, Albert, assisted him: Knight, *Robin Hood: An Anthology of Scholarship and Criticism*, page 449
164. According to Cavens: Behlmer, Rudy. "Swordplay on the Screen," *Films in Review*, June-July 1965, page 363
165. The medieval broad blades: Behlmer, *Films in Review*, June-July 1965, page 366
166. Curtiz loved the use of scenery: Ibid, page 366
167. "He has excellent form": Ibid, page 366
168. When Hill scored: Freedland, *Errol Flynn*, page 73
169. As a result, Warners' drew up: Errol Flynn legal file 3102 D USC Warner Brothers Archives
170. Al Aleborn reported, "Curtiz company called": Behlmer, *American's Favorite Movies*, page 83

Set It to Music and Send It to the Masses

171. "When we exercise the next option": Jack Warner memo to R.G. Obringer, January 19, 1938, USC Warner Brothers Archive
172. "more fervent advocate of Curtiz": Rode, page 223

173. Wallis went as far as claiming: Wallis, Higham, *Starmaker*, page 54
174. "Oh, Curtiz was a Hungarian": Reed, Rochelle, ed,, page 24
175. "Trim just a little": Wallis, *Starmaker*, page 197
176. Wallis admitted his musical tastes: Wallis, *Starmaker*, page 36
177. "Unforgettable music": Ibid, page 37
178. While working on: Winters, *Erich Wolfgang Korngold's The Adventures of Robin Hood: A Film Score Guide*, page 14
179. The Korngolds headed for Le Havre: Carroll, *The Last Prodigy: A Biography of Erich Wolfgang Korngold*, page 269-70
180. "I am sincerely sorry to have to bother you once more. I do appreciate deeply your kindness and courtesy toward me, and I am aware of the fact that you have made all concessions possible to facilitate my work.
181. But please believe a desperate man: Behlmer, *Inside Warner Brothers*, page 52-53
182. "You have to do it": Carroll, page 271
183. Blanke sent out a memo: Behlmer, *Inside Warner Brothers*, page 53
184. Within weeks his property: Carroll, page 35
185. "We thought of ourselves": Bernardi, *Hollywood's Chosen People: The Jewish Experience in American Cinema*, page 48
186. "My father was on the verge": Liner notes for the Varese Sarabande recording of *The Adventures of Robin Hood* number VCDM 704.180, June 1983
187. Film historian Tony Thomas: Thomas, *The Great Adventure Films*, page 80

188. "a textbook example": Liner notes by Tony Thomas for Erich Wolfgang Korngold – *The Adventures of Robin Hood*, Facet 8104, 1987
189. The presentation would include: Memo from Robert Taplinger to Walter Mc Ewan sent on 11 May, *Memos & Correspondence* 1 of 8 2/11/38-11/3/38' folder in the Warner Bros. archives
190. The event was held at Charles Farrell's: *Motion Picture Daily*, April 23, 1938, page 2
191. "Some of 'em hit the target: *Variety*, April 27, 1938, page 31
192. The official match was a rousing success: *The Desert Sun*, "Robin Hood Tourney Draws Large Crowd," April 29, 1938, page 3
193. On the roof of Radio City Music Hall: *Motion Picture Daily*, April 30, 1938, page 1,3
194. The mammoth marketing: *Film Daily*, February 28, 1938, page 2
195. Preparations for the pictures: *Motion Picture Daily*, April 26, 1938, page 2
196. a record number of Technicolor prints: *Motion Picture Daily*, April 22, 1938, page 2
197. "walked off the set": Lou Baum to Tenney Wright, Warner Bros. interoffice communication, February 28, 1938, USC Warner Bros. Archive
198. The studio's doctor, W.R. Meals: Higham, *Sisters*, page 73
199. "I suggest this matter be turned": Ibid, page 74
200. He flew to Miami: "Errol Flynn Plans a Yacht Trip to Nowhere," *The Evening News*, Wilkes-Barre, PA, March 18, 1938, page 20
201. The trip had to be postponed: *Evening Independent*, Massillon, Ohio, April 12, 1938, page 4
202. Two days after her arrival: *Motion Picture Daily*, May 19, 1938, page 6

203. The whirlwind tour: *Motion Picture Daily*, May 21, 1938, page 2
204. "In history of our company": Behlmer, *Introduction to Adventures of Robin Hood*, page 35
205. By four o'clock in the afternoon: *Motion Picture Daily*, May 13, 1938, page 2
206. On the west coast: *Film Daily*, May 14, 1938, page 1
207. the picture established: *Motion Picture Herald*, May 21, 1938, page 46
208. Preparations for a Technicolor: *Motion Picture Daily*, April 29, 1938, page 5
209. Geraldine Fitzgerald: *Motion Picture Daily*, October 26, 1938, page 7
210. "It is cinematic pageantry": *Variety*, April 27, 1938, page 22
211. "Excellent entertainment!" *Harrison's Reports*, May 7, 1938, page 74
212. "a richly produced, bravely bedecked": *New York Times*, May 13, 1938, page 17
213. "An apology twenty years late": Thomas, *The Films of Olivia de Havilland*, page 114

Bibliography

Aberth, John. *A Knight at the Movies: Medieval History on Film*. Psychology Press, 2003

Amburn, Ellis. *Olivia de Havilland and the Golden Age of Hollywood*. Rowman & Littlefield, 2018

Behlmer, Rudy. *America's Favorite Movies: Behind the Scenes*. F. Ungar Pub. Co., 1982

Behlmer, Rudy. *Inside Warner Brothers (1935 – 1951)*. Viking Penguin, 1985

Behlmer, Rudy. "From Legend to Film," *Introduction to The Adventures of Robin Hood*, Wisconsin Warner Bros. Screenplay Series University of Wisconsin Press, 1979

Bernardi, Daniel. *Hollywood's Chosen People: The Jewish Experience in American Cinema*. Wayne State University Press, 2013

Carroll, Brendan G. *The Last Prodigy: A Biography of Erich Wolfgang Korngold*. Amadeus Press, 1997

Curtis, James. *James Whale: A New World of Gods and Monsters*. Boston, Faber and Faber, 1998

Fontaine, Joan. *No Bed of Roses*. Berkeley Edition, 1979

Flynn, Errol. *My Wicked, Wicked Ways*. Cooper Square Press, 2003

Freedland, Michael. *Errol Flynn*. A. Barker, 1978

Harmetz, Aljean. *Round Up the Usual Suspects: The Making of Casablanca*. Weidenfeld & Nicolson, 1992

Higham, Charles. *Errol Flynn: The Untold Story*. Doubleday & Co., 1980

Higham, Charles. *Sisters: The Story of Olivia de Havilland and Joan Fontaine*. Dell Publishing Co., 1986

Higham, Charles. *The Warner Brothers*. Charles Scribner's Sons, 1974

Hill, Howard. *Wild Adventure*. The Stackpole Company, 1954

Jorgensen, Jay and Donald L. Scoggins. *Creating the Illusion: A Fashionable History of Hollywood Costume Designers*. Running Press, 2015

Knight, Stephen Thomas. *Robin Hood: An Anthology of Scholarship and Criticism*. Boydell & Brewer Ltd, 1999

Mann, William J. *Behind the Screen: How Gays and Lesbians Shaped Hollywood, 1910-1969*. Viking, 2001

Meyer, William R. *Warner Brothers Directors: The Hard-Boiled, the Comic and the Weepers*. Arlington House, 1978

McNulty, Thomas. *The Life and Career of Errol Flynn*. MacFarland and Co., 2004

Moore, John Hammond. *The Young Errol: Flynn Before Hollywood*. Trafford Publishing, 2011

Niven, David. *Bring on the Empty Horses*. Hodder, 2006

Rode, Alan K. *Michael Curtiz: A Life in Film*. University Press of Kentucky, 2017

Skal, David J. and Jessica Rains. *Claude Rains: An Actor's Voice*. University of Kentucky Press, 2009

Thomas, Tony, Rudy Behlmer, Clifford McCarty. *The Films of Errol Flynn*. Citadel Press, 1969

Thomas, Tony. *The Films of Olivia de Havilland*. New York: Citadel Press, 1983

Thomas, Tony. *The Great Adventure Films*. Citadel Press, 1976

Wallis, Hal B. and Charles Higham. *Starmaker: The Autobiography of Hal B. Wallis*. Macmillan Publishing, 1980

Warner, Jack L. with Dean Jennings. *My First Hundred Years in Hollywood*. Random House, 1965

Warren, Doug and James Cagney. *Cagney: The Authorized Biography*. St. Martin's Press, 1983

Wiles, Buster and William Donati. *My Days with Errol Flynn*. Roundtable Publishing, Inc. 1988

Winters, Ben. *Erich Wolfgang Korngold's The Adventures of Robin Hood: A Film Score Guide*, Scarecrow Press, 2007

Printed in Great Britain
by Amazon